THE RELUCTANT MEDIUM

By Margaret Pedlar

CON-PSY PUBLICATIONS MIDDLESEX

**First Edition
2005**

©Margaret Pedlar

This book is copyrighted under the Berne Convention. All rights reserved. No part of this book may be reproduced or utilised in any form or by any means, electronic or mechanical, including photocopying, recording, or by any information storage and retrieval system, without permission in writing from the publisher. Except for the purpose of reviewing or criticism, as permitted under the Copyright Act of 1956.

Published by

CON-PSY PUBLICATIONS

**P.O. BOX 14,
GREENFORD,
MIDDLESEX, UB6 0UF.**

ISBN 1 898680 40 X

PREFACE

My psychic experiences and research into the possibility of immortality have proved beyond any doubt to me that continuity of life beyond the grave does exist.

Being naturally psychic when a child held no fear for me. I was fascinated by the appearance of these solid individuals and curious as to how they could manifest their selves through the bedroom walls. They would converse with me for a few minutes and then, as I watched, slowly dematerialise from my sight.

I called them the magic people, my parents called it imagination.

Throughout the following years the psychic phenomena increased in a variety of different ways, and although I was still reluctant to accept that dead people could still be alive my curiosity prompted me to research seriously into this subject of the paranormal. If, and when, my investigations were complete, they would either give me confirmation of immortality, or I would have to dismiss all of the paranormal as imagination or creative hallucination.

Throughout these pages of my autobiography, I reveal how the resurrection of all individuals and animals is a reality, and just the commencement of a new life in a different world. I hope my truthful and genuine psychic experiences in this book will give comfort and enlightenment to many people. Seek out the truth and it will be proven to you.

Dedication

This book is dedicated with love to my son Christopher, a 'Simple Man' *, who passed peacefully into the spirit world on the 5th of October 2004.

* 'Simple Man' refers to the title of Chris' CD, recorded in 2003. The lyrics include the phrase 'I took off to find the perfect place' and it is the heartfelt wish of all his family that he has now found that place.

Acknowledgements

With love to my dear friend Anthony de Meeus for all his hard work, in trying to decipher my atrocious handwriting. Without his help, this book would not be published.

Also my love for my dearest daughter Rebecca, for giving me her encouragement and support, whilst I worked on my manuscript.

And for my cousin Leennie and her husband Peter, for their faith and confidence in me, that my psychic experiences would be published.

The names of the recipients in this book have been changed to protect their identity, also their locations for security reasons.

CONTENTS

CHAPTER 1 Page 6
About Parapsychology. Invoking the spirits and exorcism.

CHAPTER 2 Page 11
Conversing with the spirit people during my childhood. My aunt materialises to me, with a message for my mother.

CHAPTER 3 Page 18
Mother and her brother passing over into spirit, and both return to visit me in daylight.... Materialisation of spirits in the village, etc.

CHAPTER 4 Page 21
My quest for the proof of afterlife. Pythagoras and his hypothesis on immortality, etc.... My friend's husband returns to the earth plane one hour after his passing, and again after his funeral. Psychic phenomena and the fifty-four different vibrations.... About matter.... The silver cord.

CHAPTER 5 Page 24
Readings with London medium for myself, tells me of change and moving away to another county. Asking a spirit if he would like a lift in my car.... Starting a development circle, etc.... Proof of the Persian guide. Information given by Persian guide about my son's illness.

CHAPTER 6 Page 29
Kundalini, the sleeping serpent. The Pharaohs... and the Caduceus of Mercury.... The magnetic field of energy, the ley lines, etc....

CHAPTER 7 Page 32
A move away from Hertfordshire to Cornwall. Meeting more spirits and ghosts. Renting a very haunted cottage.... The corridors of time, and the difference between ghosts and spirits....Giving readings in the Cornish village, etc....

CHAPTER 8 Page 37
Dog in large manor house shows me where a boy's body lies. And spirit of a blacksmith appears to me in solid form, also tells me what happened to the boy when he was on the earth-plane. Takes me back into time, and another century....

CHAPTER 9 Page 41
My meetings on the cliffs with Daphne du Maurier, etc.... The Universe and electromagnetic waves.... Phonetic vibrations.

CHAPTER 10 Page 48
Living with spirit people in our cottage.... Proof of astral travelling.... Working in the 'haunted House'. The spirits teasing me. Talking to the spirits in Brussels.... Psychic phenomena in 'the House', and the spirits showing themselves to the Head Inspector and staff. Confirmation of their existence.

CHAPTER 11 Page 54
Our conscious and subconscious mind, and the difference between imagination and psychic awareness....

CHAPTER 12 Page 62
Reincarnation. Objects that hold vibrations from the past.... Witchcraft story from a recipient regarding black magic.... Dreams, and premonitions. My dream of Princess Diana's tragic accident....

CHAPTER 13 Page 70
Healing and its different techniques. Healing with music.... Spirit girl standing by her coffin.... The Mayans and their skills of heart and brain surgery.

CHAPTER 14 Page 77
Guide speaks about the spirit world and the different planes. The Higher Masters in spirit... and the Akashic records.... The weight of our spirit body.

CHAPTER 15 Page 82
Not letting go of a deceased person. Holding personal grief.... The Mousterian Neanderthal man and his burial rituals.... The pagans... and the persecution of witches during the 15th and 17th centuries. A true story of a witch in Hoddesdon, Hertfordshire (1912).

CHAPTER 16 Page 88
Retirement from the 'Haunted House'.... And my research into immortality confirmed.

CHAPTER 1

Parapsychology, or PSI as it is commonly called, attracts growing interest amongst people in today's world. In England alone, recent statistics showed that one in ten people are in some way psychic. There remains on the other hand a large residuum of psychic phenomena which no materialist theory has been able to explain, and I firmly believe that knowledge of the paranormal never will be complete, and perhaps that it how it should be.

There are many reasons for my belief in this. We on this earth-plane are a mixture of peoples with different religions and cultures, therefore it is our personal right as individuals to believe in, and practise, whatever faith we have or choose. Most people are content to accept the teachings of their own denomination, but there are many pathways to God whatever the religion.

Within all religions and most cultures there is mention of a life after physical death, but not much emphasis is really laid on it. In a few traditional religions it is a subject that is either taboo or not to be explored, and yet Christianity is based on a physical phenomenon. St Paul said "If Christ be not risen from the dead, then our teaching is vain, then is your faith also vain."

Amongst the countless thousands of psychic people in our world many may have gained knowledge, and proof, of the spirit world. Their proof may have come in the form of clairvoyance, clairaudience, or some unexplained occurrence has made them believe deeply that every individual does continue to survive physical death. It has brought them Comfort and hope, and inspired them to acquire more information as to how and where these unseen so-called dead abide. Much such information has been given to seekers, albeit there is also a depth of information that could never be conveyed to us as human beings of this world. However gifted we may be our brains cannot accommodate or absorb the complete picture of another living human world around us, and also, if we did have access to this further knowledge, one can imagine the chaos and disruption it would cause to all conventional and orthodox religions world wide.

For many people a person of theological standing, perhaps their local priest or vicar, can and in many circumstances does give comfort and help, particularly when a person's life has been disrupted by a chronic illness or the loss of a loved one. Also, the churches help to maintain a regulated society which offers a form of stability and order to many lives.

Albeit, most of these organised religions can be opinionated in their response to questions of the after-life. Their rigid and traditional answers do not unlock the doorway for those that seek more knowledge. In very many cases the churches are prejudiced against Spiritualism and the aspects of it. This attitude is born of ignorance. It is so easy to dismiss some thing that they have no wish to talk about, or in many cases have no knowledge of. Undoubtedly there are many clergymen of the churches and their hierarchy who are well aware of psychic phenomena to some degree, and on some occasions will be willing to exorcise a troublesome spirit from a person's home or such place, if it has become a problem to live with.

The usual procedure of exorcism is the sprinkling of holy water, oil, and the saying of prayers, hopefully to banish the 'evil' spirit. This is not always satisfactory as the haunting spirit need not necessarily be of a malevolent nature. Indeed, in more cases than otherwise, it can be a cry for help from a distressed soul that cannot understand or accept the situation he or she finds their self in.

Many other unexplained occurrences, whenever they are seen or heard, should not necessarily be classified as hauntings. It is quite a common happening when a recently deceased person from a family, or even a close friend, tries to make contact with the people they knew or loved. Communication is made to attract a person's attention. This is brought about by various means : electric lights or water taps switched on and off, or unexplained knocks, and of course on many occasions by the departed spirits manifesting themselves. Their intention is quite clear - they wish it to be known they are still alive and have survived physical death.

However, we must remember these new spirits that have entered the ethereal world have to learn how to use their vocal chords, enabling them to speak to us. This is called constructive energy. I will explain this further in another chapter.

These psychic happenings are not usually continuous. They may cease altogether after a few days or a couple of weeks, the difference being that with hauntings phenomena can be seen or heard for many years, even centuries. Newly involved souls are helped and enlightened to their new surroundings and thereby make quicker progress to further their education regarding their new world.

Albeit, earth-bound spirits will stay close to our world, often bewildered and confused in their new situation. This is when understanding and guidance should be offered them, helping them adjust to a different world. Exorcism therefore is a form of banishment, perhaps moving them on to another building or area. We must remember the earth-bound are distressed souls, perhaps the victims of a tragic accident or their passing by an unseemly bad death. Their minds and memories will still carry these bad experiences and replay the tragic scene over and over again. Some of these sad people will eventually accept help and others for some reason continue in their own privately made hell. As a practising medium, over how many years I choose not to remember, I have so many recollections of helping and rescuing these unenlightened souls. It has only been part of my work, but rewarding in the sense that I could release them from their misery.

The work and world of the clergy is more centred around the physical, their spiritual knowledge resting on theory and their holy scriptures. In comparison to persons with a theological background a genuine medium can be of valuable help and comfort to the bereaved by giving accurate proof of the continuance of life. The medium is working with an invisible and intangible substance from another dimension, i.e. the world of spirit, to obtain communication. The sensitive, or medium, will develop a higher consciousness therefore, working with higher vibrations and a quicker frequency, rather like tuning into the radio to select the station required.

A medium may have the gift of clairaudience, meaning he or she can hear speech or noises that are inaudible to other people, similar to the clairvoyant who can see the spirit people, sometimes in a solid form, and whatever else the spirit wishes to show. These two gifts can work in conjunction with each other with some mediums. The 'etherians', as the spirits are sometimes called, have to lower their vibrations to make a contact with earth people, and the medium has to raise his other vibrations and so form the interconnecting link between the two worlds.

It is an interesting fact that a natural medium can in his or her everyday life be attuned to a higher consciousness without being aware of such. We go about our usual everyday routine as so-called normal people do, except our sensitivity is heightened to everyone and everything around us. This does not necessarily mean we see or hear the spirit people all the time. It is only at certain times they make themselves known to us if it is important or necessary to help or warn us. There is never a time, day or night, that we can make them speak to us. It is, and always has been, that only they make the first contact with us.

Religious groups and the churches often speak of 'invoking the spirits'. This is untrue regarding genuine mediums.

Invoking the spirits appertains to those who are ignorant of the dangers involved in playing or experimenting with an Ouija board for instance, or an upturned wine glass on the table, and the dangers are very real. Hereby, attempts at communication will bring about contact with the lower spirits, known as elementals. They are deceased souls who have no wish to further their progress and evolve to a higher plane. With every individual, character and personality remain the same after physical death.

Consequently, like attracts like, the elementals accumulate together to cause mischief and worry, also ill-health, to experiences of this form of contact. Subsequently great concern and anxiety will always result from this practice.

Here I must make the distinction between elementals, opposed to the earth-bound. The former being of a lower intelligence will continue to remain close to those akin to their own characters. We find the same pattern on our own earth-plane, evil-doers mixing with their own kind. Unfortunately to the cost of many upright and honest citizens.

In contrast, the earth-bound spirits are on a secondary lower plane and do not cause havoc and distress to those whom they wish to contact. The reasons for creating disturbance, as previously described, are specifically for wanting to be recognised or helped.

Ignorance and prejudice tend to ignore the evidence that can be and is given through mediumship.

Spiritualism is a way of life and also a science in the fact that, as we unravel some of the mysteries of life and death, we gain knowledge of the universe around us and the many different vibrations and frequencies that interpenetrate our earth. Without these we could not exist. The very life-force within us is dependent on these vibrations to help produce our energy, like in all living things, whether they be animal, vegetable or mineral. We can understand their power when we see or feel the effect it has on oceans and currents of air, etc. Without vibrations and frequencies, power and energy would be non-existent.

We accept the effects of power as natural happenings. However, what we cannot see, hear or feel does not mean it does not exist. I am alluding now to the unseen world and dimensions around us. When we become familiar with psychic phenomena we begin to understand how the two worlds interconnect. So far, scientists have discovered and measured fifty-four different vibrations, although that is relatively a small number compared to those that are still unknown to us and penetrate the ether.

Earth people are limited in the range of vibrations they feel, unless they are very sensitive or of a psychic nature.

With our physical eyes we see our world made up of what we call matter. Everything looks and feels solid to us, although in actual fact matter has no solidity at all. Matter is constituted of atoms, electrons, protons and neutrons. Within matter, minute electrical charges move around the nucleus, as also the vibrations of electrons, and thus play their part in producing mass, or matter.

When the spirit people visit our earth-plane they pass through mass. They see this as an agitating movement of particles in and around our world, therefore having to lower their vibrations to correspond to our earthly conditions, and as we appear to them as mass they can walk through our bodies. Albeit they do not disturb our own etheric body as this is also of a spiritual nature. Having the etheric body within us we can also pass through mass if we astral travel. The silver cord as it is called (and mentioned in the Bible) is attached to the physical and the etheric body, allowing freedom of movement for the latter. If the cord should sever during travelling earthly death would occur. There have been innumerable instances given where people have spoken of their experiences of travelling the astral plane, and countless other people have witnessed this phenomenon. But I will write further on this subject in a later chapter.

Consequently, the medium can bridge the gulf between the physical and spiritual worlds.

CHAPTER 2

I was born in the year 1933 and lived in a small country village in Hertfordshire. My childhood was happy and normal, except I could see and hear people who were invisible to others. To me these were natural occurrences and they did not disturb me. My parents did not seem to be concerned by this. It was presumed by them it was sheer imagination and I would grow out of it whatever it was.

As my material life evolved, visits of these unseen people became fewer, and my life began to be caught up in the web of working for a living, and eventually marrying at the early age of nineteen. My husband had bought a small business and I had become involved in the running of this, but after three years we decided to sell the business and return to the village and the rural way of life there. My husband and I were keen to start a family, and the country village seemed to be the ideal environment for children to grow up in.

Within a few months after the sale of the business, we had bought a large detached bungalow with an extensive garden. Firmly established in our new abode, my days were fully occupied by redecorating, household chores and, weather permitting, tackling the overgrown garden.

We had been living in the bungalow for three months when I started to see the "unseen people" again. I knew beyond doubt it was not my imagination. These people appeared solid to me, but after a short time seemed to vaporise away from sight. They would make their appearance twice, or sometimes three times, a week, and on some occasions speak to me, their voices quite audible to my ears. Sometimes there was a wonderful perfume that would pervade the room. I felt no fear or anxiety, just curiosity as to why they made these visitations to me. I was to find this out the following week.

Being fully occupied in the kitchen one morning I felt a coldness around my shoulders. Turning around I saw a lady smiling at me, her manner of dress befitting the Edwardian age. I asked her who she was, and she just replied : "Give my love to your mother, she will remember me as Aunt Maggie." I wanted to ask further questions of her, but she started to fade away as if a mist had enveloped her. Puzzled I continued with my work, making a mental note I would ask my mother next time I paid her a visit.

Subsequently, when I did speak to my mother about the appearance of Aunt Maggie, she confirmed that it was correct. "She could not have been in your subconscious mind," she said. "I had never mentioned her to you as she passed over a long time ago, before you were born."

We went on to talk about the earlier years when, as a child, I saw these "unseen people". "We used to put it down to your imagination," she said, "but now I'm not so sure." Thoughtful, she paused for a moment, then said : "Albeit, it's not unheard of. Over the years there have been many reports of people seeing ghosts or apparitions. There's no answer to it, it's a mystery."

As neither my mother nor I could think of another explanation, the discussion was invariably closed. But as far as I was concerned the subject was not closed. I could not easily dismiss these visitations as imagination, because I had been given information that had proved to be correct. Having no previous knowledge of Aunt Maggie as my mother had stated it was impossible to have come from my subconscious. Numerous questions came to mind. If these people were just ghosts, apparitions or whatever, why did they look to me as solid as we humans do and were their voices audible? I could not conceive that the dead could reconstruct themselves and be amongst us again. I was reluctant to believe this was possible, and yet we are told Jesus arose from the dead and appeared to his disciples. Also, in the holy bible God says "Believe in me and ye shall have everlasting life." What was the answer? I resolved to find out.

For the next six months life went on as normal, with no more visitations. My husband was fully absorbed by his new job, and the decorating was finished in the bungalow.

Christmas was now only a month away, and the weather atrocious. Snow was forecast for the following day. I wrapped up warmly and walked to the village, as I had an appointment with my doctor. I had not been feeling too good recently but had a good idea I could be pregnant. The examination with the doctor confirmed this was correct. Exhilarated by this good news I called on mother to tell her. Of course she was delighted but gave me all the usual warnings : don't lift anything too heavy, rest more, etc, etc.

I knew of course our lives would drastically change when the baby arrived but it would be spring, time for rebirth in all of nature, a new beginning.

The weather forecast had been right. As I pulled back the curtains, the snow was falling heavily. My husband decided to leave for work early, before the roads were too bad. I closed the garden gates after he had left, and back in the kitchen made myself some tea and toast. Sipping my tea, I watched the large snow flakes falling silently to the ground. Already the imprints of our shoes on the driveway were covered by the fall. Walking through into the lounge I lit the fire and looked out onto the back garden. The expanse of lawn looked ethereal, the laden branches of the cedar trees bowed low towards the ground. The only disruption to the virgin snow was where the birds had wandered.

As I turned away from the window I heard a tapping on the small coffee table nearby. There was nothing to precipitate this noise. I lifted the table up and moved it further away. The tapping continued. Seconds later there was a whispering, but not loud enough for me to make sense of it. Four or five minutes later the tapping stopped.

'Good' I thought. 'Maybe it was the heat from the fire expanding the wood.' But a moment later I heard a loud rapping on the front door knocker. Quickly I went through the hall and opened the door. To my surprise there was no-one there. The gates were still closed, with no fresh footprints visible on the pathway. Closing the door I was perplexed as to who, or what, it could be. I had hardly turned my back on the door when the loud knocking started again. Slightly frustrated now I again opened the door. Still no-one in sight. Lifting the knocker I checked it to see if it was slack. Strongly made of cast-iron, the ring had to be manually raised to bring attention. Back in the lounge I started sorting out the Christmas cards. They would have to be posted off shortly.

A succession of loud knocks again at the door quickly brought me to my feet. Feeling a bit angry I opened the door to see a neighbour of my mother's standing there. "Can I come in for a moment," he asked, "it's important I speak to you". "Yes," I replied, "come through the lounge, it's warmer in there." Pointing to a chair by the fire I said : "Sit down. Did you call on me earlier?" "No" he answered.

His face looked serious and drawn. He paused for a moment and then said : "I'm sorry, it's bad news. Your mother has had a bad stroke. She was taken ill this morning but was still conscious when we called the doctor, but she did not wish to be taken to hospital. Just before I left her she had slipped into a coma." He went on to tell me the doctor had said she may pull out of it, "but there is nothing we can do except wait and pray." I telephoned my husband at work. He said : "Don't go round to see her until I come home. I'll leave immediately."

After our visit to mother I felt traumatised for the rest of the day. It was inconceivable to me that a person such as my mother, always active and mentally alert, could now be in a coma.

During the evening my mother's brother, John, called on us. He told us : "No change as yet, but I'll keep you informed as to her condition. I'll catch a bit of sleep now and again in the spare room. Mrs Thomson down the road used to be a nurse and we will take turns sitting with her." As he left he turned to me "look after yourself and get some sleep."

When I finally did get to bed I prayed she would make a good recovery, but during my prayers I saw a brilliant white light, with in the centre a lighted candle. Suddenly the flame was extinguished, the smoke from it drifting upwards. Intuition told me she would not survive this stroke. It was eight-thirty next morning when Uncle John came to tell us she had passed away.

The funeral arrangements were made by Uncle John and my husband. I had placed a small bunch of violets in her hands, a favourite flower of hers. Little did I know she would give me later her thanks and love.

However we still felt the void of her presence no longer with us. Christmas came and went. Now into the month of February, and there were still spasmodic falls of snow. Uncle John had asked if I would go round to mother's house, weather permitting, to empty her wardrobe etc, he would dispose of her clothes at the weekend. Calling in on my friend Winn, I asked her if she would help me, as I was not looking forward to this job.

Within two hours we had completed the task, leaving tidy piles of clothing etc on the bed. As we went down the stairs I turned around to ask Winn something, and to my amazement and shock saw my mother standing just behind Winn, an arm outstretched towards me. All colour must have drained from my face as I stared at her. Winn glanced around, but gave no sign of seeing anything.

I hurried down the rest of the stairs, and going through the kitchen sat down on a chair. Winn followed me, saying : "Are you alright? You look as if you had seen a ghost, you're as white as a sheet." "Yes, I'm alright," I replied, "just tired." I was hesitant to tell her I had seen my mother, but I had seen her, and she looked as solid as Winn or I.

Later in the evening I related the incident to my husband. "It could be a late reaction to her passing," he said, "or she came back from wherever she was to see you." Even today that appearance of my mother still remains vivid in my mind.

Our main concern now was for my uncle. For many years he had suffered from depression, owing to a wound at the side of his head that he had received while on active service. He had been stalwart and courageous over mother's illness and untimely death. As brother and sister they were close, and uncle John acted almost as a guardian to me as my father had died when I was a child. Since Christmas we had shared company with him as much as possible. However, we knew he deeply felt mother's absence.

On the twenty-third of February I was opening the morning post when my attention was drawn to a large blue light in the shape of a square. It had appeared on the dining room wall, and as I watched it disappeared and then returned twice more. Within the square I saw very clearly the face of a man. His features suggested an eastern origin. He did not speak to me but his eyes moved towards the door and then back to me. I was becoming nervous of this living portrait when it slowly faded away and I stood staring at the blank white wall.

Some time later I felt extremely cold, although the room was warm. I began to experience a sensation of choking and felt a constriction around my throat. Going through to the kitchen I sipped from a glass of cold water, but the pressure increased. Gripping the side of the sink I sank slowly to the floor, my head spinning around in circles. Panic seized me as I thought I was fainting, or even dying. It was probably only seconds that I lay on the floor. Then gradually the feeling left me and I returned to normal.

The cause of this incident was unfathomable, thinking logically. I had no pain, I felt well, so perhaps it was the unborn child that had moved or turned about. I thought no more about it and for the next hour kept quite busy with the household chores.

Opening the kitchen window a fraction for fresh air, I noticed two police officers opening the garden gate. I went to the door and stared at them. They asked my name, which I confirmed, and said "What's wrong?" The lady officer replied : "I think you had better sit down now and let us go inside." They hesitated for a moment, then gently told me : "We have some bad news for you. Your mother's brother died this morning, just over two hours ago. He hanged himself...".

He was to be buried in unconsecrated ground, but in my eyes he was not a sinner. He had been an upright, honest man, and was heartbroken at mother's death. I saw no justifiable reason why he should not lie next to mother, and expressed my strong opinions to the Vicar. He finally relented and Uncle John was buried a few days later in consecrated ground next to my mother's grave.

Late spring finally arrived and my baby son was born early in May. We called him Christopher. Life took on a new aspect for us. However, we could not erase the two tragedies that had beset us three months ago and I had neither seen nor heard anything more of the "strange" people. But I had not forgotten the events that had occurred.

The absence of these phantoms, ghosts or whatever they were did not last very long. Walking to the village one morning I made my way down a long, quiet road. On either side of the road were semi-detached houses that had been built many years ago. Next to the last house was a timber yard completely enclosed by a twelve foot high brick wall. The entrance to the yard was situated on another side road. On the opposite side of the road I noticed a man standing with his back to the wall. He kept staring at me, and this was making me feel uncomfortable.

He was wearing a check shirt and dark trousers. Age-wise, I would say he was in his early sixties. I had an uncanny feeling about him, but kept walking and watching him, thinking to myself "Is he going to make a dash over and grab my handbag?"

We were exactly opposite to each other now, when to my amazement he started to fade away. Standing still now I watched him as he became transparent and I could see the bricks of the wall through him. Then suddenly he was there no more.

Perplexed, I walked over to the wall and examined it carefully. There was no opening for him to have made an exit through. The wall was solid. And yet this man looked a normal human being so how could he vanish into the brickwork?

Still wondering over this strange experience I continued my way to the village. Prior to this morning I had never witnessed a spirit in daylight. In retrospect I asked myself was it imagination? But I could not accept this explanation. What I had seen was real. Then, there was a possibility that my mind could project thought forms to appear solid in this physical world of ours. Thinking logically, again the answer had to be no. My thoughts had been concerned with the morning's shopping. I now began to wonder : could it be conceivable that there was survival after death, and if as human beings we are indestructible how can our bodies regenerate to become solid again? Many questions arose in my mind and I needed to find indisputable evidence and proof, if only for my own compos mentis.

During the evening I related the experience to my husband. He listened intently to me.

"Well," he said, "I know you are not prone to imagination. What you saw must have been authentic. Most people have heard of ghosts or spirits, but not everybody can see or hear them, and remember you had similar occurrences here in the bungalow. The only conclusion I can come to is that you have extra-sensory perception, you are a natural psychic."

He went on : "What I don't understand is why you are so sceptical about an afterlife actually existing." I thought for a moment. "It's not that I'm sceptical," I said, "just reluctant to believe that when people die they can reconstruct their bodies and minds again resembling what they were on earth. Also I'm a realist and I cannot conceive how they can use energy and function without nourishment or oxygen."

"I can't answer," he replied, "the only way is to research the subject, ask people like the Spiritualists, visit their churches or see a medium."

We had to conclude the conversation, as it was well past midnight and both of us were too tired to think.

Five days later, by a strange coincidence, I was buying milk in the dairy shop when unintentionally I overheard part of a conversation between two ladies. The younger lady was quite emphatic that she had definitely seen a man fade away into a brick wall down Milestone Road. Her description of the man identified with mine.

It was now an opportune moment to retie my shoe lace as I heard the elder lady reply :"Don't worry, dear. He has been seen many times by several people. He haunts that part of the road. He is Mr Browning. He died in an accident years ago, before you were born."

Mentioning to my husband part of the conversation I had overheard he said : "You certainly could not have imagined the man if other people have seen him as well. You have gained proof of that today."

An outstanding account of a materialisation in broad daylight was related to me by a personal friend who left no doubt in my mind as to the authenticity of her story. It concerns one such elderly lady called Daisy Turner.

Every village has its well-known characters and ours was no exception. My friend Christine Wray was on week-end leave from the Women's Royal Air Force. Whilst walking down the lane to the village shops, she saw Daisy approaching from the opposite direction. "Hello Chrissie !" she shouted, waving her stick.

Christine did not have time to stop and talk, so she waved back, calling to her "Hello Daisy !", and took a left turn down a convenient side street - although she felt mean for avoiding the old lady.

When she returned home she told her mother about the encounter. Her mother immediately replied: "I know you didn't see Daisy Turner because she has been dead for two years !" Christine was very shocked at the news and had to sit down with a cup of tea to recover.

When Christine came to see me she said that because she no longer lived at home she had no idea that Daisy had died. Her mother told her that, if it was any consolation, several other people in the village had also seen her wandering around near where she used to live.

A most fascinating fact is that many of these materialised spirits can use their vocal cords so that their words are audible to our ears. Also their brain and memory continue to function as on the earth-plane.

CHAPTER 3

My quest for researching the proof of an afterlife began when I attended a Spiritualist church in our nearest town. I was pleasantly surprised to find a relaxed and hospitable atmosphere amongst the congregation. The elderly lady medium gave many communications purporting to come from the spirit world. I listened intently as the recipients affirmed her messages. I could not substantiate their answers as all of these people were strangers to me, but after the meeting closed I was offered a cup of tea and spoke to the gentleman in charge of the meeting.

I asked whether the medium lived locally. "Oh no", he replied, "she comes from London and gives clairvoyance here once a year."

Pursuing my train of thought I then asked :"Is it possible she has some prior knowledge of this congregation?" He laughed. "No that's impossible! She visits churches all over the country, and she would have to have an extensive memory bank to remember every person. Also, the details she gives - and before you ask me, she is not a mind-reader. As you heard tonight, futuristic events were foretold to many of the recipients and at a later date they will prove to be correct."

"Are you a newcomer to the Spiritualist movement?" he went on to ask. "Yes", I replied, "I wish to know more about death."

He surprised me by his reply. "There is nothing more to know about death. When the physical body has expired life always continues. Death is only a transmigration of the soul or spirit body within us. Keep searching and you will find the truth. But remember - there are excellent mediums, and many that are indifferent when giving a reading. Sort out the wheat from the chaff." It was good advice and I intended to do just that.

Aware of my growing interest in psychic phenomena my husband bought me a newspaper and placed a weekly order for it. It was called "The Psychic News". I browsed through it and found much enlightenment on this subject. A large number of Spiritualist churches were advertised, not only in the British Isles but also overseas. It made me realise just how many people were interested in the afterlife. Also of great interest were the readers' letters, describing some of their own psychic experiences.

But I knew I had to gain my own personal knowledge if I was to achieve my purpose in proving the hereafter. Reflecting, I thought about my own experiences and the accurate, previously unknown, information I had received. The subconscious mind had to be ruled out, and I had no previous knowledge. I asked myself whether a continuum of intelligent life-force was conceivable, how and where did it exist. But as this thought progressed through my mind it opened up many more avenues of reflection. Logically thinking, how could a dead person reconstruct again into a solid life form, complete with its faculties including an intelligent brain and memory? Could there be a rational answer to this phenomenon?

I came to the conclusion I had to continue with my search, keeping an unbiased attitude of mind. And so I became a member of our local library and procured two books : "Parapsychology" and "Metaphysics". I read them with voracity and found both volumes interrelated, with a similar aspect on immortality and psychic phenomena, but with diverging opinions on the existence of an omnipotent deity. These were apparent in both books. Metaphysics, I found, is concerned with the nature of existence and the origin of matter and mind, also the interaction between them. It is concerned with matters relating to the psyche, i.e. the human soul, spirit or mind. It brought into my perspective the relationship of free will, personality and our inner and outer selves. However, parapsychology gave me a deeper understanding of the functionalism of the mind and the subconscious. I found myself reassured as I read about extrasensory perception, mediumship and mental concentration, all of which work independently from the recognised channels of sense.

Pondering over our natural five senses I could only conclude that there is a strong possibility that all human beings, and animals, have these latent extra senses. In genuine clairvoyants these extra senses would be active at times, enabling them to perceive and hear psychic phenomena. Albeit, many thousands of people at times, although unaware of any existing psychic sense, do see and hear things that are not physically or mentally accountable for. In these cases, the psychic sense that has been lying dormant has been activated.

The large majority of people when they experience some form of psychic phenomena presume it is their imagination, without giving much thought or speculation as to how or why such an occurrence could happen. This could be born of ignorance, or caught up in the progress of their own material life. But the interesting part of this is that imagination stems from the thinking part of the brain. For instance, if a person was told that a particular house or place was haunted, the imagination could produce a thought form, because the brain has received a mental message and therefore tries to reproduce the thought in reality, similar to an artist who sees in his or her mind's eye (or imagination) a picture he or she wishes to paint. So what is real or unreal? The proof of a psychic occurrence is when we have not been thinking prior to the vision or sound. To clarify this point : if we could produce phenomena of vision or whatever by thought alone, then it would be possible to see or hear our so-called dead relatives and friends any time we choose. Therefore, when the dormant sense is activated, usually the person has been in a passive state of mind, similar to the medium who has attained a higher state of consciousness. Development of these extra senses can or may be taught under correct tuition.

The hypothesis of telepathy, telekinesis and hypnosis differentiates from the psychic work because it influences the mind via will-power. Telepathy is communication from one mind to another, and hypnosis a semi-sleep condition induced by willpower on a person, or persons, who are susceptible to suggestion, whereas telekinesis is the movement of physical objects. These are all forms of applied energy to, or from, the mind.

Belief in immortality is common to virtually all cultures and religious traditions. Most of the ancient philosophers identified a supernatural union with God in an afterlife. Pythagoras taught the kinship of all life, immortality and the transmigration of the soul. Pythagoras was, and still remains known as, a brilliant mathematician, but he was also a master of sciences and ancient wisdom. Amongst his teachers were the priest scientists of ancient Egypt, also Zoroaster the founder of the Persian Magi sect. The framework for his hypothesis was that the soul and body are intrinsically distinct substances which coexist during our life but separate again at death. Plato, as a theologian, was an expert on the divine, the eternal, the immaterial and the intelligible realm. He presented explicit proofs whenever he introduced it into any discussion. It makes us realise that these ancient and learned men were more familiar with knowledge of the afterlife than the majority of people today. If I am correct in assuming this I can only conclude that they would embody a non-materialistic approach to life, as they regarded their physical bodies as temporary abodes of the soul.

There had been a heavy frost overnight, and as I drew back the curtains the trees and grass were sparkling in the early morning sun. I noticed a large spider's web had been spun over a rosemary bush, the intricate gossamer threads reaching out to its perimeter. 'Similar to my world', I thought. With every thread of knowledge gained I was reaching the outer edge. To where? The invisible and intangible world of spirit.

CHAPTER 4

It was the second week in November, and apart from a few heavy frosts at night the sun still gave off warmth around midday. I picked up the morning's post and casually looked it over: the electricity bill, a gardening catalogue and a letter from Christine. Christopher had gone back to sleep for a while, so taking advantage of these few quiet moments I made a cup of coffee and opened Christine's letter. Half way through the second page I felt a coldness around my head and shoulders. I could see nothing that would account for this change in atmosphere but I distinctly felt an indefinable presence as though someone was watching me.

Finishing my coffee and my letter I went back into the warm kitchen. Friday was baking day for me, and as it was becoming increasingly difficult to cope with Christopher's demands once he was up and about I started to work on the pastry. Suddenly, the icy coldness came around me again. I shivered. 'This is crazy', I thought, 'here I am in a very warm kitchen but feeling like a block of ice

Speaking to myself I said : "What's the problem this time? Who is it?" Very clearly I was answered with three words : "Margaret, it's Tom." I tried asking more questions but there was just silence.

Returning to the pastry I pondered over who it could have been. The only Tom I knew was in London attending a meeting with his firm. His wife Patricia had mentioned this to me when she had phoned last week. Suddenly I realised the icy coldness had gone, the room temperature and I were back to normal. Christopher was now fully awake so there was no more time to reflect on this strange incident.

The rest of the day went smoothly, except for the occasional tantrum from Christopher - the start of teething problems I presumed. My husband Ron arrived home later than usual. "Damn car was iced up before five o'clock", he said. After our evening meal we played with Christopher for a while until he was tired, and then settled him down to sleep.

"There's a good film on television tonight", Ron said. "I wouldn't mind watching it if it doesn't disturb your reading." "Go ahead," I replied, "you know what I'm like once I get absorbed in a book, oblivious to anything or anyone around me." Just at that moment the phone rang. "Answer that before it wakes Christopher up"! I said.

Opening my book I sat down on the settee. I could hear the murmur of Ron's voice, it sounded serious. After six or seven minutes he came back into the lounge. "It's Patricia, she wants to speak with you. It's bad news. Tom's dead, he collapsed at the hotel in London with a heart attack Wednesday morning."

Patricia told me : "Tom is being brought back from London on Monday. I'm sorry I could not phone you earlier but there has been a lot to do, you know, arranging things." "I know", I said. "If there is anything we can do to help let us know, won't you?" She was very tearful again. "Just come to the funeral. It's been arranged for three o'clock Tuesday at St Mary's Church."

Over the weekend Christopher had developed a cold and was irritable with the teething problem. I phoned Patricia and explained the situation: "Ron will stay at home with Christopher but I will be there. I'll join you at the church door".

Tuesday morning arrived. By the time I backed the car out of the drive the overnight frost had cleared, and given way to brilliant warm sunshine. Turning left off the busy main road, I drove down the narrow country lanes until I came to the village, if it could be called so - more like a hamlet, with its small clusters of thatched cottages and one shop-cum-post office. The village green with its circular duck pond was the centre piece for this quaint setting.

A sharp turn left by the village inn brought me into open countryside. I continued along another small lane. The hedgerows on either side were flanked with hemlock and the orange hips from the summer briar roses. In spring and summer the church would be partially hidden from the road by the oak and ash trees, but now most of their leaves had departed from their branches and lay like a bronze and golden carpet on the ground.

I parked in the space provided for visitors that was in close proximity to the church and walked through the small lychgate. Glancing at my watch the time was only two-fifteen. Placing my spray of roses and freesias in the porch of the church I wandered around the old churchyard. A solemn quietness surrounded me. Young and old lay here, for most of them the difference of the time span on this earth would be the only thing they shared. I sat down under an old yew tree for a while, pondering on the mysteries of life and death. Why should the very young die so early, and for the aged what did they learn from their experience of life, each one of them carrying some trauma, perhaps pain, physical or mental, each one of them in their resting place, whether it be a grand memorial or the narrow mound of overgrown grass? A tortoiseshell butterfly alighted close to me, basking in the warm sunshine. I smiled to myself : what a similarity, even this beautiful butterfly had undergone a metamorphosis. Its chrysalis left behind, it was free in a new world.

I was rudely awakened from my thoughts by the tolling of the church bell. Collecting my flowers from the porch I stood by the door, the vicar and I exchanging a few words as four black cars came slowly up the driveway. I followed the procession into the church to sit at the back.

From the windows shafts of sunlight filtered across the aisle. The monotonous voice of the vicar droned on, giving us no illusions that there was a life hereafter, and yet what I had seen and heard from the spirit world was a reality with proof. Can people only blame their own minds for living in ignorance?

The service closed with a hymn, and after the interment we made our own way back to Patricia's mother's house for tea. The curtains had been drawn across the windows, as was the tradition in respect for the deceased. The best china tea-service was being used today for this sad occasion, and an assortment of sandwiches and cakes laid out. Groups of two or three people had gathered together, speaking in quiet voices of Tom. I made no mention of hearing Tom's voice. I knew Patricia, also her parents, would have frowned upon the subject as they firmly followed the traditions and doctrine of their church.

As I said goodbye to Patricia and company, a shimmering white light appeared behind Patricia. I stared at it for a moment. Tom's face was in the centre of it, still the same old Tom with a hint of laughter in his eyes. His sense of humour he had obviously still retained.

CHAPTER 5

A short time after Tom's funeral Ron suggested that I visit a medium at the College of Psychic Science for a personal reading. "It may prove interesting for you. I can take a day's leave as I am still owed some holiday time," he said.

I had previously told him I had seen Tom after the funeral, and expressed my doubts as to whether it could have been my imagination as it was an emotional occasion. "Difficult to judge under those circumstances," he replied.

A week later I phoned the College of Psychic Science in London and was fortunate to obtain an appointment for a reading with a medium, a Mr Bo-Goran. The appointment was booked for eleven-thirty on the Thursday. I was slightly apprehensive as to what the outcome would be from the reading, but I felt I needed some practical research as well as my continuous reading of literature.

On the Thursday, leaving the car at the village station, I caught the nine fifteen train to King's Cross. The train was twenty minutes late arriving in London, so I hired a taxi to Queensberry Road. As the taxi weaved its way through the busy metropolis I had a feeling of nausea. "Tension", I thought, but it disappeared by the time I stepped into the relative quiet of the College.

When I met Mr Bo-Goran I presumed he was of Scandinavian nationality, because of his slight accent, albeit his command of the English language was excellent. He opened a door into a large sunlit room, with comfortable armchairs and a well-worn carpet. Making a gesture for me to sit down he sat opposite to me and asked:

"Have you had a reading with me before?" "No" I replied. "Firstly I must tell you a lady came into the room with you. She is your mother and passed into spirit two years ago. She gives her love to you and wishes to thank you for the bunch of violets you had asked to be placed in her hands before she was laid to rest." This I confirmed.

He then went on to describe my mother as if he was looking at her photograph. He was accurate in every detail. He continued: "You have seen her yourself shortly after she passed over, haven't you?" I nodded my head. "She also has a brother called John with her in spirit, he passed by his own hand." This also I affirmed. "A gentleman called Tom wishes to be remembered to you. Had a sudden death, heart attack. He tells me you attended his funeral the previous week."

Throughout the hour's reading more information was given to me. As he had nearly finished the reading he predicted I would have another child, a daughter, next July ! "You are a psychic yourself," he said, "develop your gift and use it wisely to help others."

In spite of the accurate information I had received I was still considering whether he was an astute mind reader. But on reflection, it was true he had predicted several events for the future. Would they prove to be correct? I said to myself:"Time will tell."

Could it have been spiritually designed that I shopped for my green grocery on Friday instead of Saturday? The proprietor was of Polish nationality, his personality congenial. During the procedure of serving me he laughingly asked me if I believed in ghosts. Before I could reply he told me the lady he had served prior to myself had mentioned she had seen her deceased husband a few days ago. "Funnily enough", he said, "I believed her. I myself had some strange unexplainable incidents during the war while I was working as an undercover agent for the British Intelligence. I'll tell you about it some time."

"I would like to hear about that", I replied, and tentatively told him I was doing some research into the subject and hoping to form a development group in the new year. "Well, you can certainly count myself and wife in", he said, "let me know when it's to start." Within the next two weeks I had acquired five eager sitters, ready to join the circle. Our group would consist of seven people, including my husband and myself. However, for the time being, there was much to think about as Christmas was only two weeks away.

Driving the car into the comparatively large new town of Stevenage I bought most of my Christmas groceries from Sainburys, excluding the fruit and vegetables. Unashamedly, I felt no guilt buying two large Christmas puddings, as I really could not find time to make them. Christopher, once awake, would occupy most of my time.

On the way home there were intermittent flurries of snow. Switching on the windscreen wipers and changing gear to ascend the steep hill into the village, I was surprised to see old Mr Clements standing on the pavement. Giving a quick toot on the horn I pulled in against the kerb. He smiled and lifted his hand to me in recognition. Leaning over to open the door I called to him:"Get in ! I'll give you a lift back into the village." But as I spoke to him Mr Clements slowly disappeared into a vaporous like mist. Perplexed I closed the car door again and sat for five minutes or more to meditate on this uncanny occurrence. I had heard no mention of Mr Clements passing over, our village like many others was susceptible to gossip of any kind. Well, I thought, when an opportune moment comes along I would make some conservative enquiries. Automatically I put the gear lever into first again and made my way home.

The following week I made an appointment to see my doctor. I had been feeling nauseous for some time - better get it cleared up before Christmas arrives. He diagnosed pregnancy, "early July", he said, "or a bit later." Laughing he added:"Never know with babies, arrive when they feel inclined." Delighted with this good news I recalled Mr Bo-Goran's words: "You will have another child, a daughter, early July next year."

Christmas came and went, with no discernible happenings from spirit. I telephoned our prospective sitters for the circle and all agreed Friday nights would be ideal to sit for one hour. I had previously gleaned a little information on how to conduct and organise a development circle, always to open and close with a prayer, asking for protection around each sitter. Apart from that information we hopefully would find our own way and be guided by spirit.

A few days later, while preparing the evening meal, I saw a lady opening the front garden gate. Wiping my hands I went to the door. It was Mrs Thompson. She did a lot of good work raising funds for various charities.

"What are you collecting for now, Mrs Thompson"? I asked. "It's for Dr Barnados Homes", she replied, "and our ladies are holding a dance in the village hall Saturday night to raise more funds." "I don't know about the dance," I said, "but I will certainly give you something now."

As I went to get my purse a sudden thought crossed my mind. Mrs Thompson was the next door neighbour to Mr Clements. Using discretion, I firstly asked after her health. "Not too bad," she replied, "but this cold weather doesn't help my arthritis." I was sympathetic with her. "And how is Mr Clements these days, stays in the warm I suppose."

She frowned at me. "Didn't you know ! He died four years ago." "No I didn't," I said. "But I have only been back here in the village two and a half years."

She went on to tell me Mr Clements had been accidentally knocked over by a car, and died at the side of the road before an ambulance could be called. "Yes", she said, "it was very sad. It happened just before he walked up the hill to the village." I felt it would be incongruous to relate my experience of offering him a lift when I saw him a few days ago.

The Friday night development circle had now been in progress for eight months, except for a two week break as my daughter was born the eighth of July.

Within the first month of sitting we became aware of spirit presence. A strong eastern perfume permeated the room, which all of us could smell. In the second month the phenomena increased. Large blue lights moved around the room. These lights could not have come from an outside source, as the heavy velvet curtains were closed across the window,

We used two table lamps, each with a forty watt bulb, so the room was illuminated enough for us to see each other quite clearly. The phenomenon was only transitory but it occurred every Friday night, the blue lights alternating in size. I asked myself: were these illusions, created ourselves by energy drawn from our bodies or minds? But if this was so, this phenomenon would be common-place amongst ordinary social groups.

As autumn approached the intensity within the circle increased. On a few rare occasions the lights would be absent, but a different phenomenon was now taking place. Although I was feeling comfortable and relaxed I felt as if I was drifting away into a subconscious state, at the same time aware that my face was stiff, rather like a mask had been placed over it. As this was happening I also experienced a strange sensation from my solar plexus, as though cotton wool was being gently pulled away from me. Whispered voices brought me back to a normal state. When I opened my eyes the other sitters asked me if I was alright. "Perfectly alright", I said. "Why?" They told me they had all observed my features change, also another pair of eyes superimposed over mine that were firmly closed.

Discussing this new psychic event after the circle we came to the conclusion transfiguration had taken place. Consequently, we were in agreement that we should seek some professional advice to find out what was happening.

Tuesday of the following week I rang the College of Psychic Science and asked if it was possible for someone to attend a Friday night's sitting with us to confirm whether this was genuine transfiguration. I was asked to write a letter to a Mr Horace Leaf, c/o the College of Psychic Science, with my enquiries, and it would be passed on to him as soon as he returned from America, which would be in two weeks time.

When the letter from Mr Leaf subsequently arrived he proposed to visit us Friday the following week. Would we please confirm by phone that this would be convenient. He would travel down to Hertfordshire by train and arrive at six o'clock at the village station, also thanking us for the cheque we had enclosed in reimbursement of his time and expenses.

Mr Leaf was a distinguished gentleman with an extensive knowledge of parapsychology. He asked no questions of us, but during a small meal he shared with us he spoke of the various psychic experiences he had witnessed in England. He was conversant with all aspects of psychic work, and there was no doubt in my mind that Mr Leaf would be genuine and honest with his investigation of our development circle.

In the lounge Mr Leaf watched us arrange the upright chairs, close the curtains and switch on the two table lamps. He then proceeded to take the pulse of each one of us, and jotted down his findings in his notebook. "I shall sit on the outside of the circle", he said, "to observe just what is happening. Please relax and forget I am here. Proceed as you normally do each week. Half-way through the sitting I shall quietly walk around to each one of you to take the pulse rates again."

During the hour's sitting I again felt the energy being taken from my solar plexus, and the mask-like sensation over my features. The strong eastern perfume pervaded the room. I could faintly hear whispered voices, their conversation incomprehensible to my ears.

After the sitting Mr Leaf discussed with us what he had seen and heard during the hour. He told us my features had changed twice. "Firstly", he said, "a Persian guide is your control, and will use you for trance work to speak through you. The second guide is an Egyptian. His purpose, or work here, is for helping to produce materialisation by drawing the ectoplasm from your solar plexus. This ectoplasm has been witnessed tonight by myself and the rest of the sitters. This will be a powerful circle."

He spoke to us of the correct breathing exercises we should practise within the circle to allow Kundalina (the sleeping serpent) at the base of the spine to unfold and release the psychic energy into the pineal and pituitary glands (in a later chapter I will explain this in more detail).

I jotted down his recommendation of various books on ancient religions. "You will be surprised", he said, "how closely related the many religions are in connection with our knowledge and proofs of immortality." Referring again to our circle he suggested we should place a tape-recorder near by to record any words spoken in trance, also a pair of reliable scales. "Each one of you to weigh yourselves before and immediately after the circle has closed. The amount of weight loss will determine how much energy has been used from you all, but it will be replenished within one hour."

He concluded his talk to us by explaining that during the hour all pulse rates had been normal except mine, which had slowed down almost to non-existence.

Mr Leaf's wisdom and knowledge gave us the inspiration to continue with our circle. He was not surprised when I told him I had no wish to become a medium. "You have no choice", he answered, "one way or another they will work with you, reluctant as you may be. Please remember one does not have to have faith to believe in immortality, it is an accepted fact by many people today and in the centuries past. Many religions display a diversity of beliefs and practices, but Spiritualism, or belief in immortality, can and does furnish the proof of the survival of earthly death."

CHAPTER 6

I had no fixed ideas in my head that afterlife was a certainty, but now I had to find rational explanations as opposed to the supernatural. But when no other reasonable alternatives presented themselves I had to conclude there must be another dimension with human intelligence other than our earth-plane, and so I was starting to realise that what I had experienced so far of this intangible, unseen world was just the tip of the iceberg. How much more valuable knowledge lay submerged in the depths beyond our normal range of the five senses? And if there is such an extension of life after this one, where, and how, does it exist? The questions in my mind were innumerable. Our developing circle could be the key to unlock the door between the two worlds.

Two months after Mr Leaf's visit, we were starting to obtain excellent results within the circle. I realised I was slipping away into a subconscious state, with strange feelings in my throat as if someone was trying to speak through me. Towards the end of the year I was falling into a deep trance every circle night. I had no knowledge of what had occurred until after the circle, when the tape was played back.

The doorkeeper guide had given his name as Saraheeda. He spoke of some of his life on our earth-plane, and also told of where he used to live in Persia. The sitters were told they could ask questions, personal or otherwise, and the answers the guide gave were always accurate. His information on the afterlife was very instructive.

The second half of the hour's sitting, sometimes longer than the hour, would be used for withdrawing ectoplasm to produce materialisation of a spirit person, or some form of phenomena for everyone to witness. On one occasion the sitters told me after the circle they had watched a fully materialised Chinese gentleman walk the length of the room and then vaporise.

Although not in any doubt about the information the guide gave us, we agreed it would be interesting to confirm the name of the place 'Palav' where Saraheeda said he had lived in Persia. Consequently, one of the lady sitters wrote to the Persian Embassy asking if such a place did exist. Her query was answered by letter a few days later, and it confirmed that in ancient days Palav was a district of Persia, the name Palav having been changed many years ago. Persia, as it was called, is now of course named Iran. Gradually we obtained proof of what Saraheeda told us, also his prognostication of future events.

It was becoming apparent to me that the gift of clairvoyance was increasing in my daily life, and I was getting accustomed to seeing, and hearing, these people from the astral plane, having accepted the fact that there had to be an interaction between our world and spirit. On several occasions when my husband had to stay on longer in the evenings at work, I would hear my name called. I would walk through to the hall to investigate this adult human voice, half expecting to see a person from spirit, but the hall would be empty except for an indefinable presence close to me. This human voice could not have been imagination since Christopher also heard it. He would call out to me: "Mummy, who was that calling you?" I would ask him: "What did you hear?" His answer was always the same:"A lady called your name 'Margaret' ". I had good reason to think it was my mother who had paid us a visit but was unable to manifest herself to me.

For quite a lengthy time neither Christopher nor I heard the voice, but something else strange was occurring. My husband and I would hear Christopher laughing and talking to someone, while in his bedroom. I would go into his bedroom, lest he should awake Rebecca. I would ask him:"To whom are you speaking, and why are you laughing?" His answer was always the same: "A lady comes to play with me and makes me laugh".

This was a mystery but it was to be solved, as I found out two months later. Heavy rain one morning kept us indoors. To amuse the children I opened a box of photographs and told them to find a place to fit them into the album. Christopher had taken several from the box, but was focussing his attention on one in particular. I asked him: "Shall I tell you who that is?" "I know", he said, "this is the lady who speaks to me, and makes me laugh when I go to bed." It was a photograph of my mother.

I wondered if there was any significance in why she paid such attention to Christopher. I gave this quite a lot of thought, and a feeling of concern clouded my mind. Discussing the situation with my husband, he suggested Christopher should have a check-up with the doctor. The doctor diagnosed a hole in the heart. Consequently we made two visits to Westminster Hospital so that various tests could be made on him, and an operation on his heart was scheduled for early spring.

I had read in "The Psychic News" of a spiritual healer in Tottenham, London, and took Christopher to see him for healing every week for four months. He responded well to the healing, sleeping well, and with a large improvement in appetite, but unfortunately Mr Fricker could do no more to repair the defect in the heart. Although my husband and I tried to stay optimistic we felt secret doubts as to the outcome of the operation.

One night I had a dream, which I believed to be a psychic indication in relation to my son's forthcoming operation. In my dream I was looking at a coloured picture of a stormy sea. A small vessel was tossing about helplessly amid the high waves. My eyes focussed on the frame of the picture. It was sturdy and strong. My interpretation of the dream was unequivocal. There would be a rough passage for my son's recovery, but his frame was strong enough to withstand the turbulence. I made no mention to Ron about my dream, thinking perhaps my subconscious mind was being prompted by anxiety.

The circle was held as usual Friday night. During the session Ron had asked the guide if he could furnish any information with regard to Christopher's forthcoming operation and recovery. Listening to the tape after the session I heard Saraheeda answer Ron's questions:

"In our world we are aware of your anxiety for your son. The operation will be successful, but the after-effects will cause much concern for you for several hours. It will be decided amongst the medical staff to administer a new drug to your son. Even using this they cannot be sure of his earthly survival, as this new drug will be used for the first time. Have faith in what I have told you. Your son will survive this trauma and his body will respond to this drug. Also, his recovery will be complete."

Hearing this information on the tape we should have felt relieved and uplifted, but under conditions of anxiety and stress the human tendency is naturally to be the prey of doubts and fears, and I was aware that negative thoughts contain the seeds of self-destruction. If the guide was incorrect with his answers to Ron's questions, not only would I have to re-evaluate my belief in afterlife but abandon all thought of continuing my research. On the other hand, if Saraheeda's message was correct, this would be the ultimate proof of an intelligent entity that had given accurate and prior information far beyond the realm of my subconscious mind. Such were my thoughts as I awaited the day of the operation.

The operation was over and it had been successful, but on our arrival at the children's heart ward we were not allowed to see him. The consultant told us Christopher's condition was serious. Blood clots had formed and were causing him to have fits after the heart operation. He said: "We are now going to inject your son with a new drug that has not been used before. It will be several hours before we can be certain that he is responding to it." He advised us to go back home and rest, telling us we might telephone as often as we wished throughout the night. "The staff will keep you informed of his condition."

We could not rest as our minds were in turmoil, but Ron reminded me of Saraheeda's prediction: "So far he has been correct, even as to the new drug they are using." We phoned the hospital on every hour. The fits were becoming less frequent. Finally, at eleven thirty p.m. we were told: "Your son is fully recovered, the drug has worked. You may see him tomorrow."

A week later, visiting Christopher, the ward-sister told us that prior to Christopher's operation unfortunately they had lost two children under the same blood-clotting condition.

CHAPTER 7

With the food we eat, and cell growth, the process of metabolism in our bodies produces the vital energy, or life force, within us. We are familiar with our own energy, and perhaps aware of other peoples' vitality. Most of us accept as factual the natural energy around us in our world: the magnetic field of energy that lies beneath the earth and oceans, the energy of the sun and also the elements that produce the weather conditions. It would be a difficult task to enumerate the many various forms of energy that are invisible to us. What we perceive from energy are just its effects.

Perhaps unknown to many people is the powerful energy of Kundalini, also referred to as the Sleeping Serpent. It is the seat of psychic energy, and resides in the centre of the base of the spine, enclosing the channel of the central nervous system. When awakened by psychic development it rises through the chakras, eventually reaching the pituitary body and pineal gland. Certain mystical and occult phenomena are connected with the functioning of these glands. Transcendental meditation can help to facilitate the awakening of the Kundalini, but great care should be used if practising by yourself. It can be dangerous, and leave you open to obsession as you are projecting your conscious mind onto a subconscious level. It is advisable to be under the supervision of a knowledgeable tutor of Yoga who would guide you through the correct techniques of the breathing exercises. Interruptions of any kind, the telephone ringing or loud knocks on the door, can force the conscious mind and Kundalini to rapidly return with undesirable results, or the astral body could be separated completely from the physical body, resulting in heart attack or death.

Kundalini is not only recognised for the development of the occult arts, it is a timeless source of energy and wisdom. The Pharaohs of Egypt wore the symbol of the Ureas snakes entwined around their head. This represented to them the energy and wisdom of the hermetic arts. The Caduceus of Mercury (as it was known to the Romans) is shown as the symbol of medicine. The central rod is interlaced with two serpents, and the small ball at the top of the rod is the pineal gland. The wings at either side of the pineal gland represent the mythical Greek God Hermes, the messenger of God. Again it symbolises energy, wisdom and healing.

If one could glimpse through the mists of ancient times it would be possible to understand and piece together how the birth of the earliest religions came into being. Most religions derive from a common origin, the resurrection from physical death. Long before Biblical times, ancient people had observed manifestations of spirit and were aware of another existing world close to ours. These psychically endowed people were familiar with trance states, precognition of future events and every aspect of the occult arts. So valuable was the information they experienced and witnessed that they thought it important enough to transcribe.

Over four thousand years ago a tablet of baked clay was found in Sumeria. The writings were inscribed in cuneiform characters as they are called. The Epic of Gilgamish, when it was translated, disclosed incredible information in regard to their seances. Participants would gather together for the seance on ground they knew to hold magnetic energy. The ground was regarded as sacred - later to be known as sacred ground.

The magnetic fields of energy are interrelated with psychic work as they increase the frequencies of vibrations to the medium. The energy, or power, drawn from the medium for the psychic work is produced mainly from the solar plexus, also known as the sacred. And so these mediums or prophets were obviously acquainted with the earth's energies that could help increase their perception of the esoteric world.

Through the succeeding centuries many books have been written, with the theme of afterlife based on factual proof. Regarded with esteem are such books as "The Egyptian Book of the Dead", the Hindu "Bagar-av-ad Gita", also the Kabbalah and of course The Holy Bible. We read in all of this literature a repeatable pattern of the psychic arts.

In the Eastern world, before the predate of Biblical times, rituals and ceremonies were being practised at the meetings of these psychics. Mysticism was introduced into the temples that were beginning to be built. During their rituals they used the word 'God', as it was an ancient Hebrew word for power. They experienced visions not only of their ancestors but other spirits who gave help and advice. They were under the illusion that these strangers came from a higher source or plane. They called them Gods and Goddesses. This was the early beginning of polytheism (the worship of many Gods and Goddesses). Not only had this credence been accepted and worshipped, but over most parts of the world paganism expanded. Idols were created and erected to the deities. Many of these were the fruit of imagination. The phenomena of weather conditions were attributed to these Gods. The sun God Apollo was worshipped in Greece because the sun ripened the harvests, bringing health and well-being into the peoples' lives. In Norse mythology we read of Thor, the God of thunder and lightning. Thor was feared, presuming his wrath was directed to them for some misdemeanour. Wayside shrines were built where prayers and gifts were offered to appease the deities.

Places where visions had been seen, or voices heard, were also regarded as sacred places of healing. We are familiar with the stories of Lourdes and the miracles of healing that have taken place there, but pilgrimages were made to many such places for help or healing.

Before Jesus was born there were many prophets. In the Holy Bible we read of Moses, 9th century B.C., leader of the Israelites. On Mount Sinai he received from Jehovah the ten commandments. Elijah, 9th century again, was another great prophet, and after Elijah, Elisha. At Christmas time we are reminded of the three wise men who prophesied the birth of Jesus. Jesus, being one of the greatest healers and prophets, was called the Son of God. Christianity began with the teachings of Jesus Christ. At the age of thirty he began his mission of proclaiming the Kingdom of God. Monotheism, the credence that there is only one God, is still observed today in most parts of the world.

With conventional religions, belief is in an omnipotent deity, or the Trinity. In today's world there are of course many offshoots of religion, but most people have conceptual values regarding their own faith be it what it may, and the majority of people with their personal faith and prayers derive from a common source: the continued existence of the soul, or spirit.

Every religion is the effect of psychic phenomena dating well back into the early centuries. How strange it seems to us today that churches and various places of worship tend to ignore the fundamental foundation of original prayer and worship of our distant ancestors. I do not for one moment suggest these places of worship should indulge in meetings for clairvoyance, seances etc., and in all fairness and honesty I believe the churches and chapels do give a certain code of ethics for people to try to live up to in their daily lives. Spiritual guidance and upliftment are generally given to people who seek help. All these things are spiritually good for the well-being of mankind.

Proof of an afterlife cannot be given in any conventional church or chapel. We may listen to sermons on the resurrection of the physical body, and the prospects of living in heaven if we are good, or of damnation in hell if we are bad.

Many parts of the Holy Bible are controversial regarding an eternal life. In some chapters of the Bible we read that the dead shall stay dead until the last trumpet call, other pages relate the physical body shall have everlasting life. Bearing in mind that the Bible had been transcribed by many people over a great age, their own personal thoughts and experiences of the resurrection from physical death led to conflicting opinions on this subject.

In many places of worship today there is ignorance and intolerance of psychic work. Personally I cannot understand the aggressive attitude towards genuine mediums for their work. To preach an afterlife and condemn mediums for their gift, be it healing or clairvoyance, is to deny the truth of what they preach: the existence of an afterlife, the spiritual healing of Jesus, the clairvoyance of the great prophets and the phenomena of the miracles and materialisations, all of which we read about in the Bible.

The credence and practice of Spiritualism is a natural religion, also a science born free of doctrines and dogmas. I can only assume that the reason why these ecclesiastics are prejudiced against all aspects of Spiritualism is due to their ignorance, leading them to classify them as the work of the devil. If they were to investigate further into the occult arts they would realise that genuine mediums do not indulge in the black arts of devil worship, or the practice of table rapping or the Ouija board. These are not in keeping with the work of sincere and honest mediums.

It would be a comforting thought that maybe in a few years to come the churches would combine with spiritual healers and mediums to work in conjunction with each other for the benefit of mankind as the ancient prophets and healers did many centuries ago.

Over the years I have found the atmosphere in most churches to be peaceful and uplifting. The many prayers that have been offered to God, or an infinite power, have condensed into an energy of tranquillity and love.

It was not surprising then for me to learn that some of these buildings had been built on a magnetic field of energy, generally known as a Ley Line, but to my delight a major piece of the jigsaw puzzle fitted into place when I noticed carvings on old chairs and doors, and incorporated into the plaster and stonework, representing the serpent Kundalini, the seat of psychic energy, and the symbol of healing and of the hermetic arts.

Over many years the serpent has been wrongly represented as evil. The Bible relates the story of Adam and Eve in the Garden of Eden. Eve tempted Adam to eat an apple from the tree of knowledge. Sexual ability and practice equate to the tree of knowledge. The tree of life is represented as the spinal column in the human body, enclosing the nervous system and housing the Kundalini. The forbidden fruit for which Adam was tempted were the secretions and substances for the procreation of human life.

When you are developing your psychic powers you will experience the awakening of Kundalini. You feel an intense concentration of energy in the sacrum area at the base of the spine. This vital source is an expression of the energy of creation, and the vital force of existence. Not only were the ancient prophets familiar with this source of energy within their bodies, but also different cultures all over the world carried this knowledge of the serpent power.

However, I must stress here that this serpent power was not used for sexual gratification, but for the purpose only of allowing this energy to reach the pineal or pituitary glands, therefore bringing about psychic development.

It is a misnomer that the serpent has been labelled as evil. This is owing to the misuse of its power within the Satanists and black arts groups. This force is a reality, and therefore should be used at all times with care and guidance.

In this chapter we begin to see parts of the picture as the pieces of the jigsaw puzzle fit in, the energies within ourselves interrelating with the earth and cosmic energies, each one playing an important part in bringing together mind, body and spirit.

CHAPTER 8

The year was 1970 and five years had elapsed since I had sat for a personal reading with a medium.

It was a pleasant spring morning when, acting on impulse, I made an appointment with a well-known medium, a Mr Joseph Benjamin. Although I had no particular reason for my visit, there was a restlessness within my mind and body that I could not account for. Knowing I should be satisfied with my material and spiritual life, I tried to analyse these inner feelings of discontent. I had no problems with the children, they were both healthy, happy, and attending the village school, my husband was fully employed with the prospects of future promotion next year. So why this turbulence of unrest that surrounded me?

When I finally met Mr Benjamin, I found he was totally different to what I had expected. I had expected him to be similar to Mr Bo-Goran, a quiet and unassuming person, so I was surprised when this small jovial gentleman opened the door and greeted me with "Hello love! Come in." The reading with him was very evidential and correct, punctuated with his sense of humour.

I had never had a reading with Mr Benjamin before, but had read and heard much about him and his demonstrations of clairvoyance at the Wigmore Hall, London. Towards the end of the reading he told me: "There is unsettlement around you, in your mind, and very shortly in your environment. Don't worry about that," he said, "it will be all for your good. You will be making a big change that will be of great benefit to you and your family."

He then went on to tell me that we would be moving away. "I can't tell you exactly where you are going but it's lovely countryside, a bit hilly, and I can see water around this county on three sides." I was puzzled by this statement of his, as neither I nor my husband had ever thought of moving away from our quiet village. I told him this, but again he was emphatic that we would move, and before Christmas of this year.

Before I could speak again he went on: "I see you and your family moving into temporary accommodation. It is a cottage with two front doors that open straight out onto a pavement, a bus stop is immediately outside. But you will be moving into a home of your own just before Christmas of next year!" I wanted to ask questions but he waved his hand to silence me. "The house I see now is large with gardens on three sides, and the view I see from the house overlooks a beautiful valley." He finished the reading saying: "Life is sometimes like a valley, has its ups and downs. Take life as it comes!"

Travelling back home I felt pleased with most of the reading, but completely confused about his prognosis of moving. We had no reason to move. Discussing the reading with Ron during our evening meal, he was amused when I told him Joe Benjamin had foreseen a move for us to another county. "Well," Ron said, "I'm sure he was wrong there. I don't see any reason why we should want to move, we are quite content where we are. Besides, we have to consider the children, who are settled in school."

We gave it no more thought. But in late spring, the first signs of predestination started to manifest themselves when earth-moving equipment was brought into the surrounding countryside, churning up the fields with an expediency that surprised everybody. Within a few months, foundations were laid for new housing estates, and before very long the new houses sprang up almost like mushrooms overnight. Country lanes were demolished, and in their place came a cement maze of wide roads, sign-posted to different parts of the the estate.

This enormous change in our rural environment was due to an overflow of people from London wishing to resettle in new homes, with employment of which there was plenty. The tranquillity we had enjoyed for years was slowly but steadily vanishing, never again would we see the golden cornfields with the wild red poppies and blue cornflowers growing amidst them.

Progress gives way to change, and has to be accepted for better or worse. The change was obviously going to be good for the newcomers, as the new estates when completed would almost link with the fairly new shopping town of Stevenage, also the large factory area, but leaving a green belt between the two.

Ron and I did not feel resentful against the newcomers moving down to Hertfordshire, only sad to see the rural countryside we had loved since childhood change so drastically. A few years ago there had been rumours of new sites that might be built, but we never dreamed that they would cover such an extensive area.

Property in our village was rising in price rapidly, and we heard of many people born in or near our village selling out and moving to a different part of the county or further afield. Surprisingly enough, one evening Ron brought up the subject of selling our bungalow and moving. For several weeks we constantly discussed the advantages, and the disadvantages, of uprooting ourselves from our home.

We finally reached the conclusion we would take the plunge and move away to more rural, and quieter surroundings. We chose Cornwall. Ron spent a week phoning estate-agents in Cornwall, enquiring about rented accommodations for the winter. Within a fortnight we had several replies to our queries. But many of the winter-let cottages we thought would be too isolated for the children travelling to school, or Ron to work, if that could be obtained.

We were starting to get concerned now as autumn was fast approaching, and several good offers had been made for our bungalow with its half acre of land. We accepted the best offer and duly made arrangements for our furniture to be placed in store for the winter. Maybe it was coincidence, but the following week another letter arrived from one of the Cornish estate agents, informing us that a cottage with reasonable rent was available immediately until Easter of next year, the cottage being situated in a small village between Fowey and the town of St Austell. Without any delay Ron phoned the estate agent and booked the cottage, posting off the deposit the same day.

We stayed with a friend overnight, and the next day made an early start on our journey to Cornwall. I clearly remember that day. There had been a hard frost overnight, the bare branches of trees looked as if they had been coated with icing sugar. Early as it was that Saturday morning, a few cars were already on the main road, but moving slowly over the icy surface.

When we stopped in Somerset for an early lunch and stretched our legs the sun had burst through, and it continued to shine as we finally entered the county of Cornwall. We took this as a good omen that all would go well with us in our new environment. Now and again we caught glimpses of the sea, but did not stop, telling the children we would have a closer look perhaps tomorrow. It was early evening by the time we had reached the small village, and found the cottage that was going to be home to us for a few months. The evening sky was interspersed with colours of yellow and rosy pink, the promise of a good day tomorrow, Sunday.

Three or four plump ladies were standing chatting next door to the cottage we were renting. They viewed us with curiosity. Ron turned off the engine and we looked at the cottage. Quietly he said: "Do you realise that Joe Benjamin's prediction about the cottage is absolutely correct? Look, the bus stop is here near the pavement, just outside the cottage window!" I froze. "Blimey"! I said. "But which cottage is the rented one?" He laughed. "All of it, don't you see. It must have been two separate cottages at one time, and they are now made into one: there's the two front doors onto the pavement, plus the two downstairs windows."

Getting out of the car we stood for a moment looking at the cottage. One of the plump ladies waddled towards us, her ample bosom resting on her stomach. "Good Hevning", she said with a broad Cornish accent, "you be the people renting this here cottage?" "Yes, are you the lady with the keys?" Ron replied. "I be that", she said, passing over two keys. "I thought t'was you when I see the two chil' with you! The owner of the cottage has gone out tonight, says she will call in to see you on the morrow." With that she waddled back to her friends for probably more gossip.

The interior of the cottage had been modernised to some extent. The bathroom and toilet were fairly up to date. Two small bedrooms lay on the same side as the bathroom, with one double room facing the street. We called it the green room, as the decrepit looking wallpaper was dark green as also the tattered carpet covering the floor. The downstairs rooms were not much better, the furniture aged and old-fashioned. The small sitting room consisted of an old sofa, three armchairs and an old fashioned sideboard that leaned forward as we walked towards it. "The floor is uneven," said Ron, "so be careful in this room."

The adjoining room had no interior door. It was another double bedroom, the large bed taking up most of the space except for a small table with a wash basin and jug on it. Again the decor was dark and dismal. "We shall have to sleep down here in this room," I said to Ron, "because I can't sleep in that awful green room upstairs, it gives me the creeps!" "I don't mind," he said, "but we will have to keep these curtains closed over, as this room overlooks onto the pavement, also this door must be kept locked all the time!"

The kitchen, we found, was not too bad, just basic, but there was a fridge (working), a small kitchen table, four chairs and an ancient stone sink next to the gas cooker. I smiled at Ron. "Bit archaic, isn't it, meals will have to be pretty basic."

"Talking of meals, what are we having for tea tonight?" Ron asked. I glanced at my watch. "Eight fifteen! You're out of luck, I forgot the shops will be closed now to buy anything !" "Never mind," Ron said grinning, "I'll try begging down the street." Before I could say another word, he opened the front door and walked off. Ten minutes later came back with four parcels of fish and chips. He said: "I noticed the chip shop round the corner as we drove into the village".

Two hours later we settled down to sleep, our first night in Cornwall. But my thoughts went back to Hertfordshire. I should miss my friends, also I was sad at having to disband our Friday night circle. My quest for proving the afterlife would now be abandoned. I wondered now in my sleep state: had it all been imagination, or perhaps the subconscious mind, that could produce life-like human beings? Mentally I told myself: "The ghosts have gone, they are in the past." But were they?

CHAPTER 9

We had lived in the cottage for nearly three weeks and adjusted quite well to our new surroundings. Although I was taken up with the daily chores of washing, shopping etc, I still found time to go out walking by myself and explore the countryside around. My husband was fortunate to obtain employment a few miles away at Bodmin and the children settled in a school at Fowey.

Despite the time of the year the temperature was almost spring like, and Christmas was only three weeks away. I would walk through the narrow lanes leading to the beach. Primroses and dogtoothed violets were out in full bloom, apparently quite normal for this county. The sea always fascinated me with its various colour changes. On some days it would be aquamarine, on others a dark blue or steely grey. Climbing a path upwards over the granite rocks I would walk along the cliff top. The small coves far below me with their pristine sands were inaccessible to human beings. It was here that I always felt a fusion of mind, spirit and body. In solitary silence I would sit watching the energy of the sea and feel the energy of the air. Kundalina would arise from the base of my spine, perhaps awakened by these natural forces, and rejuvenated by all these energies I would slowly make my way back home.

On one of these occasions a lady was walking down the field that adjoined the cliff top. Her small dog ran towards me barking. She called to me:"He is quite friendly, he won't hurt you!" As I stroked her dog she came up to me and asked if I was on holiday. "No", I replied, and told her we were renting a cottage for the winter and hoping to buy a property in the new year. We conversed for a few minutes and then parted company. As I walked homewards I had no notions that I would meet or converse with this lady again. It was many months later that I learnt of her identity. She was the well-known authoress, Daphne Du Maurier.

I had only seen Mrs Kenton once to speak to. One morning she knocked at my door and asked me if I had such a thing as an 'honion' Perplexed for a moment I repeated her request, 'an honion?' "That's what I did say," she said. "Of course ! Come in," I replied, and gave her two onions.

Mr and Mrs Kenton were pensioners and I guessed they found it difficult to get by on their weekly pension. I told her she need not replace the onions, and she thanked me profusely. From my kitchen window I noticed how she would walk to the washing line. Throwing a child's skipping rope up and over the line, she would then stand on the skipping rope, enabling her to peg out the washing. I would smile to myself at these clever antics of hers. Picking up the skipping rope she would then waddle back indoors, leaving her washing blowing high in the air, including the three pairs of voluminous knickers that now looked rather like inflated balloons.

It was on a Wednesday evening and I was preoccupied with cooking the evening meal when Ron came home from work. I made a cup of tea for him, and he told me he had to go to London the next day on business for the firm. "I will be back some time Friday evening," he said. A hotel room had already been booked for his overnight stay. "Will you be all right?" he said. "Of course", I replied, "just be careful on the roads."

Thursday evening both the children had washed and were settled in bed by ten o'clock. I settled down to read a couple of chapters from a novel. Feeling tired by eleven, I looked in on the children. Both were asleep. After I had washed quietly in the bathroom I checked all doors were locked and climbed into my bed downstairs.

I had no idea of what time it was, when I was awakened from my sleep by a strange noise. Switching on the bedside lamp, I saw an elderly woman standing at the side of the bed. I sat upright, staring at her in amazement. As I took in her appearance I judged her to be in her early seventies. She was wearing a coloured pinafore over her dress, her eyes dark and brooding set in a face that was thin and lined. Several clips held her grey hair in place. She did not speak to me, but I seemed to be the object of her curiosity. I felt no fear of her, as the room was permeated with a benign ambience. I asked her - "Who are you?" She answered with one word: "Flo". And within seconds a cloud of white mist had enveloped her, and she vanished from sight.

Sinking back onto the pillows I thought about this strange encounter, and resolved to tell no one about it. My husband quite likely would suggest that I had been overtired, or imaginative. For the rest of the night I slept deeply, without dreams or any disturbance, but in the morning the memory of the apparition remained clear in my mind.

Friday morning I caught the bus into the small town of St Austell to shop for a few extras for Christmas, buying food and a few more presents for the children. Also I chose, and paid for, a small television set that was to be delivered the next day.

The children were on holiday from school. I had left Christopher swatting up on some homework, and Rebecca was spending the morning with a girl friend from school. Arriving back home later than I intended I placed my purchases on the kitchen table, asking Christopher if he had eaten any lunch. "Yes", he replied, "I bought a pasty from the corner shop." "Well", I said, "Dad will be home tonight, and we will be having steak, chips, and how about these large mushrooms I bought in town?" He was quiet and did not answer me. "What's the matter?" I asked him, "cat got your tongue?" He smiled at my question.

Helping me put the groceries away in the cupboard he suddenly asked me: "Mum, have you ever seen an old man in the cottage, playing a mouth-organ?" "No, I haven't", I said. "Have you?" "Yes, this morning while you were in town." He then went on to describe an old man standing half-way up the stairs, wearing an old string vest over his trousers. He was playing a mouth-organ, but he was playing the same tune all the time. I asked Christopher: "Do you remember the tune he was playing?" "Yes", he said, "it was 'Silent night, holy night' After he stopped playing the mouth-organ, I went upstairs to see where he had gone. I looked in all the bedrooms and the bathroom, but there was no one there." Christopher looked at me inquiringly as if I could supply the answer to this mystery, which of course I could not. Luckily Ron walked in, back from London and our conversation returned to normal. Christopher never mentioned the mouth-organ man again, as excitement was at a high. The thought of a television arriving tomorrow put all other thoughts out of his mind.

Christmas week arrived and a small series of unaccountable events occurred: loud knocks on the kitchen table and, after the children had gone to bed, the television was switched on again after we had switched it off. Constantly we felt cold breezes when all the doors were closed. There was no mistaking that indefinable preternatural forces were present.

With the excitement of Christmas Day we were preoccupied with the unwrapping of gifts, television and the preparation of dinner. We spent the afternoon walking on the beach, removing our coats as the weather was more like late spring than mid-winter.

For the rest of Christmas Day and the following two weeks there were no further appearances of Flo, nor of the mouth-organ man. I thought to myself, maybe they have disappeared for good. But I had been wrong in assuming that, as it was not too long before they made themselves known to us again on several occasions. Also, I was to receive information on their earlier lives in the cottage.

Mrs Kenton came round to see me one wet morning, holding a large umbrella over her head. I invited her indoors and offered her a cup of tea. "I've been wondering", she said, "if you would like me to show you how to make pasties tomorrow?" "Thank you, I would like that," I replied. "Tell me what ingredients we need and I will buy them later on today."

The next day Mrs Kenton arrived at ten-thirty for my lesson in pasty making. She asked me to peel the potatoes and turnip, while she cut up the tender meat. "While I'm ashowing you," she said, "I'll make one for meself, and one for my hubby, if you don't mind." "Please do," I replied.

As we worked at the table she chatted on about how she and her hubby had enjoyed their Christmas, and what they saw on television. When the pasties were ready to go into the oven I made a pot of tea for us. She was quiet for a few moments, took another sip of her tea, and then, staring hard at me, she asked: "Are you alright here in the cottage?" "Perfectly alright, why do you ask?" I said. Pausing for breath a moment she then went on:"What I do mean, you not been affeared of anything, strange things I do mean?"

I knew exactly what she was getting at, and taking a long sip of my tea I smiled at her. "Oh, you mean the spirits? Yes we are well aware of them but they do not trouble us." She now leaned forward, and almost whispered to me: "Tell me, what did you see?"

And so I related to her the appearance of the lady I saw in the bedroom, describing her in detail but omitting the name she had given me in answer to my question. "That's right", Mrs Kenton said, "I know well who you did see." Before she could speak again, I said: "She told me her name." "What's she say it was," she asked. "Flo," I said. "Well I be blowed, you be right."

I went on to tell Mrs Kenton about the gentleman Christopher had seen and heard, but did not describe him to her. "Oh, that was Flo's hubby, All. He died before her, always wore an old string vest over his trousers winter and summer alike, never happy unless he was aplaying the mouth-organ. Only knew one tune, 'Holy night, silent night.' Got on my nerves sometimes. You must be physic!" I laughed. "It's called 'being psychic'" "Oh well," she said, "same thing I suppose."

Removing the cooked pasties from the oven, she asked whether I could see anything or anyone around her. "Do you really want to know?" I asked. "Yes please", she said. Wrapping her two pasties up to take home, I told her I had seen a small child, a girl, standing close to her. Her name was given to me as Rose.

Mrs Kenton turned away from me for a moment, she was wiping her eyes. "Are you alright?" I asked. "Yes my dear", she said, "but thank you for telling me that. I lost my little girl years ago. She died of an illness. I called her Rose. It's made me happy today to know she lives on."

Confirmation about the spirits in the cottage gave me much food for thought. Was it just coincidence that I should be involved again in a psychic stream of information stemming from an unseen source? And once again, despite my reluctance to accept this as the answer, I felt I had now to pursue my quest into the research of immortality.

In this small parochial Cornish village news travelled fast, and Mrs

Kenton lost no time in spreading word of the latest events. Myself, plus the clairvoyance we had discussed, made exciting gossip for her to talk about around the village. I was made well aware of this when I went to shop. A few people would stop talking as I walked by, others stared at me and said 'Good morning'. The Celtic people I found to be gentle, but very superstitious. And with many villages partly mediaeval I wondered whether they regarded me as a witch, or an alien being.

However, although the villagers viewed me with ambivalence, I sensed an underlying curiosity amongst them. And so it did not surprise me when a few days later Mrs Kenton came to speak to me in connection with my clairvoyance. Would I be so kind as to give her neighbour Mrs Dunstan 'some of my clairvoyance' as she put it? I agreed to give Mrs Dunstan a reading, and told Mrs Kenton not to divulge to me any information regarding this lady. Within a month the requests for readings became frequent, and word of them began to spread beyond the village and further afield.

Finishing a reading for a lady one day she asked me whether we had found a suitable property to buy. "No", I replied, "we have been to various estate agents, but nothing as yet has appealed to us." She told me her daughter and family were moving to Scotland, and their house was about to be put up for sale. "Go and have a look at it," she said.

The same evening Ron and I located the house. It was at the end of a small lane on the outskirts of the village. The house was large and detached, with a garden on three sides and overlooking a scenic valley. It corresponded accurately to Mr Joseph Benjamin's description during my reading with him. Within eight weeks, with the legal transactions completed, the house was ours, and we moved in a week before Easter.

It was not very long after moving in that readings for people resumed. I was obliged to keep an appointment book, but never asked for surnames or peoples' locations. A private reading for each person would last for one hour, at the end of which the clairvoyance would automatically cease, which was extraordinary as I had no time-piece with me in that room. Over the next five years I gave numerous readings, including to holiday makers who had made enquiries about any local mediums available. I recall one gentleman who came for a reading, and who told me afterwards that he was the President of a well-known London Spiritualist Church. I found it interesting to meet people from all walks of life, complete strangers to me. On one occasion, giving a reading to a lady, I thought her face looked familiar but I could not recall where I had seen her before. After the reading she told me of her vocation, she was an actress.

As time passed, change came into our lives. Both children had left home, studying at different universities, Christopher reading chemistry and

Rebecca archaeology. But I was still kept busy. Apart from the private readings, I received many queries by 'phone asking if I could investigate haunted premises. These events I always found fascinating, with a variability in the hauntings. What most people do not realise is that there is a difference between spirits and ghosts.

Spirit people are deceased human beings who at some time existed and inhabited the earth-plane. When earthly death takes place the silver cord breaks away from the physical body, and the etheric body is free of its physical shell. The silver cord is mentioned in the Holy Bible (Ecclesiastes XII). The duplicate human form remains the same in its new surroundings, called the astral or spirit world. Spirit people still retain their minds, memories and intelligence, and although their bodies are lighter in weight their astral world appears to them as solid as ours does to us. The atmosphere that surrounds them is also lighter than ours, their vibrations are on a higher and quicker frequency, and so by lowering their vibrations to adjust to earth conditions they can manifest themselves to us. When we realise that solidity is only a matter of degree we understand how it is possible for the etheric people to penetrate into our heavier world. These atmospheric conditions are made clearer to us when we watch on television astronauts interpenetrating space.

There are of course spirits which are earth-bound and for various reasons choose to stay in the environment they have been used to on earth. For example, people who die suddenly by accident or violent death cannot at first come to terms with this new situation they find themselves in. Trying to communicate with their non-psychic relatives on earth can be bewildering and frustrating. Physical pain or discomfort is not experienced in the spirit world, as pain applies only to the physical body. The spiritual body can neither be harmed nor destroyed. Being closer to our earth conditions many of these earth-bound spirits can manifest themselves and stay close to the location where they met with an untimely death, linked with the memory of the occurrence. Therefore, a spirit is a living soul or person, in comparison to a ghost which is a transparency of the past.

From time immemorial there has always been perpetual movement in the universe. Within our universe, electromagnetic waves create a constant rhythmic cycle of movement that radiates into a pathway of energies, forming a gridwork similar to a gigantic spider's web. The earth and ourselves are ruled by these cycles and rhythms, as also our life force. Trillions of vibrations operate in the universe, many of these are known to us but are invisible beyond the ultra violet and infra red. As these invisible electromagnetic waves rotate our earth under a frequency control and photon, images of people or events are captured in a web of time. And as all time is simultaneous, this astral projector can reproduce pictures of a previous existence of people, or events and places, from hundreds of years ago. Because the gridwork in the universe is so enormous the chances of one vibration in a trillion recapturing images on earth are once in every five years.

Phonetic vibrations are transmitted on a quicker frequency, the auscultation reaching the images prior to the visionary. A transparency of the original event will remain visionary for only a few moments. The most recent occurrence of this phenomena was witnessed in the county of Devon in 1998 by a dozen hikers walking across a field. They all heard music, speech and laughter. They watched in amazement as a picture formed of a bygone age. A country fair was in full progress, the participants in it being dressed in the mode of an earlier century.

Therefore, ghosts or phantoms are an image from the material past, similar to a cinecamera with the scene replayed. These visual reflections are known as 'the corridors of time'.

CHAPTER 10

The pursuance of my research into immortality was now starting to formulate a pattern that made me realise that I was obtaining factual evidence of an intelligence beyond my mind. This unknown informant was giving me information that neither I, nor the recipient, had any previous knowledge of. Therefore telepathy, mind reading and imagination all had to be eliminated.

For my own peace of mind and reputation the authenticity of what I had seen and heard had to be verified. Consequently, when recipients had no prior knowledge about a certain event, or such, I had seen or heard, I would ask them if they could make discreet enquiries to confirm this. They were willing to do this, if only for their own curiosity.

I recall an interesting example of one reading that proves the point of an unknown agency relaying information to me from another dimension. One evening I was giving a reading to a lady previously unknown to me. The spirit of her mother stood behind her. Describing her mother I told the recipient: "Your mother passed into spirit ten days ago." "That is correct", she answered. I went on to explain the health condition her mother died from. More information during the hour was also verified. Towards the end of the reading I had a psychic vision of the resting place where the mother had been buried. The grave had been made up with soil and was covered with fresh flowers. I saw a youngish lady, a gentleman by her side, standing by the grave. The lady unclasped a gold chain from around her neck, removing the gold cross that had been attached. Putting the chain into her coat pocket, she then proceeded to push the gold cross into the soil at the head of the grave. The reading then finished.

I asked the recipient if she had understood what I had given her. "Yes", she replied, "you gave me accurate information concerning my mother, but I cannot accept the latter part you gave me. You see, my husband and I were the last to leave the churchyard." On this she was adamant.

As I walked to the door with her I asked if she could discreetly make enquiries as to whether anyone else had placed the cross in the grave. "I certainly will", she said, "it's made me curious now. I'll phone you if I find out."

But she didn't phone, she did better than that. Five days later she called on me. "I've brought my sister to see you and explain what she told me yesterday." I invited them through to the lounge and the sister then related her story to me.

"When my husband Bill and I left the churchyard there was a small group of people talking to the vicar. We were all to meet up at my sister's house for tea. Driving back to the house, I said to Bill 'Please turn back, I want to leave something for Mother.' I think Bill thought I was over stressed, but he did take me back. Everybody had left and we were alone. The grave had been filled in with soil, all the flowers placed on top. I then took the chain and put it in my coat pocket, the gold cross I pushed into the soil at the top of the grave. I did this as Mother was religious, and I wanted her to have a cross with her until the grave was properly made up. Bill and I were the only people who knew this."

Remembering another fascinating event of a bygone age, I think it is worth a mention. I received a phone call from a gentleman, asking me if I could pay a visit to his home on the outskirts of Bodmin in connection with a haunting of many years. As it was mid-winter I did not relish the thought of making the visit by myself. However, he agreed readily to my request as to allowing my husband to accompany me.

It was a large manor house situated in a few acres of land. The gentleman invited us in and gave us coffee while he explained what he and his dog had seen over a number of years. His story is as follows. "I have stables in my grounds that have been unused for many years, they are empty but always kept locked. There is only one window, and that is upstairs in what used to be the hayloft. On most days it is my habit to take a stroll around the grounds with my dog, passing the stables on my way. Quite often I see a face at the window looking at me, sometimes I see this face three times a day, other days it is not there at all. There are only two keys to the stable, and I have them here always on my key ring. I cannot count how many times when, on seeing this face, I have unlocked the stable door and gone up to the hayloft. On every occasion I have found no one in that room. Now the strange thing is, as soon as I unlock the door to go in my dog makes for a corner in the stable, he looks up at the hayloft, and then runs outside to a small piece of ground close to the stable, the hackles raised high on his back. He repeats this every time we enter the stable."

I listened carefully to his story, and when he had finished speaking I proceeded to ask him logical questions. First of all I said: "Have you considered the question of reflections on the window that may be creating the likeness of a face?" "Yes, I have", he replied, "but there is nothing nearby to cause a reflection." The second question I asked was: "Do you take your stroll at the same time of the day?" "No, the times vary as I have business matters to attend to."

"This last question", I said, "concerns your dog." Discreetly I asked him: "Do you think your dog senses a small animal that has tunnelled through to the corner of the room from outside?" Again he answered: "No. I have investigated that possibility myself, even dug into the soil outside where the dog runs back to. You will see for yourself when I take you down."

After this process of elimination from natural causes it seemed reasonable to suspect that a supernatural force was operating within and outside that building. He switched on the outside lights, also the interior one to the stable, and as he paused at the stable door he said:"Now watch the dog closely." The dog ran quickly across the concrete floor to a corner, and then stood still for a moment, looking upwards to the hayloft. Without warning he suddenly ran out of the door. Quickly we followed him. With hackles up, he was standing looking down on the piece of ground the gentleman had told us about.

The dog's repetitive behaviour was certainly puzzling, but as we entered the stable again he remained quiet and docile. My husband, the gentleman and the dog stood by the now closed door, the gentleman holding a notebook ready to write down any psychic information I might receive.

With my psychic senses heightened I slowly paced the empty floor. Suddenly I felt as if I had descended to a deeper level. A smell of scorching and heat surrounded me. Now in semi-trance state, I could see the interior of the stable had dramatically changed. It was as if I had gone back into a bygone age. The floor was now composed of large flagstones, the heat was emanating from a small furnace. Judging from the horse shoes and various tools I realised I was in a smithy. My assumption proved to be correct, as a large man walked towards me. He was wearing an open necked shirt, the sleeves rolled up showing his strong brawny arms, also a long leather apron that practically covered his knees. His countenance was kindly, and I felt no fear.

I asked him: "Were you the blacksmith here?" He answered: "Yes." I continued with my questions: "What is your name and where did you live?" He gave his Christian and surname, and told me he used to live in one of the cottages on the estate.

"You have been seen many times looking out of the window in the hayloft, is it because you have no wish to leave the forge?" "'Tis not me that stays here", he said, "'tis the boy." "What boy?" I asked, "tell me about him". Intently I listened as he told me he had unofficially adopted a boy aged five, his parents having died in an accident. "Having no children of my own", he said, "I grew very fond of him. He loved to watch the horses being shod, and the bales of hay pulled up by rope aloft. He wasn't supposed to go up in the hayloft, I told him often enough. He was nearly seven when he died, fell from the loft and broke his neck". "Where did you bury him?" I asked. He pointed to the wall. "Close to the wall near the bush. Couldn't bury him proper like in a churchyard as he was never christened. But the dog sees him and knows where he lays."

I could ask no more as the blacksmith started to dissolve into another dimension, and I returned out of the semi-trance from a few moments in time, distant by two hundred years.

The authenticity of this psychic investigation was proved when the gentleman asked if we could visit him again. Apparently, he had discovered valuable information relative to my previous visit, he also had photographs that would be of great interest.

The result of our visit to the manor again was enlightening. Sitting in the drawing room, the gentleman first of all showed us six photographs, each one a picture of an old forge - three taken inside, the other three outside. He explained to us that his father, many years ago, had taken these photographs of the old forge. "After my father passed on," he said, "I had the forge altered into a stable. The original stones were left as they were, but the level of the floor was raised by two foot and cemented over."

Opening his note book he then proceeded to tell us he had made a search in the county archives at Truro. The blacksmith's name and address were correct as given to me, the date when registered being 1803. It is always mentally rewarding when receiving authentic feed-back from any psychic work.

The gentleman recipient was pleased with the result of the investigation. Afterwards I explained to him why the boy could not make contact with the blacksmith. As a result of a sudden death it is quite usual for a person to be confused and disorientated. This is is called being earth-bound. The boy would stay close to the place where the blacksmith spent most of his time. Neither the blacksmith nor the boy could make contact with each other, each existing within different boundaries. As a medium I could make contact with the blacksmith but could not help the boy until he had accepted mentally that he no longer existed on the earth-plane. He then would be released from earthly life. There was a strong possibility that he would be enlightened by our visit.

I think it is important to emphasise the fact that of the many spirits that are so-called earth-bound not all are confused by the transition from physical body to spirit. The majority of spirits are well aware of their new surroundings and for a time prefer to stay close to the people or place they loved. Their main reason for this is to try to prove their survival from physical death and hopefully alleviate the absence and sorrow their friends or family still feel.

It is not unusual for non-psychic people to be aware of aromas around them that the departed spirit previously used or was familiar with. Other phenomena can be electric lights switched on or off, also the recurrence of footsteps distinctly heard that cannot be accounted for. The purpose of these forms of phenomena is to call attention and create awareness of a supernatural energy that is still in existence.

Over the years I accumulated considerable evidence from various people who have experienced different forms of psychic phenomena other than spirit forms. The stories that I have taken more seriously are from people who claim they are not psychic or tend to disbelieve in another existence. One such person I have known since childhood had lost her husband Bill. He had passed over with a sudden heart attack. Three years after he died I went to stay with her for a week. She had no idea I was psychic and I had never discussed afterlife with her, as I knew she was sceptical about Spiritualism. And so I was very surprised one day when she told me that quite often she smelt tobacco smoke in the house. She herself had never smoked nor drunk alcohol.

I suggested to her the cigarette smoke probably drifted through a window or door from outside. but she insisted it could not possibly be that, as she lived too far away from other houses for smoke to infiltrate into her home. She then went on to tell me that as she lived alone it was her habit to go to bed early and read for a while before switching the bedside light off.

"Three or four times a week," she said, "I smell the cigarette smoke, the same brand that Bill used. I have even seen wafts of the smoke drifting across the room." "Do you think it could be your imagination?" I asked. "No", she replied, "I know it's Bill"

Towards the end of the week I awoke early one morning. I could smell tobacco smoke. Standing at the end of my bed I very clearly saw Bill. He was smiling and smoking a cigarette. "Hello there!" he said. "Hello Bill!" I replied. "She knows you are around still."

My investigation in a house at Padstow proved to be a desperate attempt on the part of a deceased mother trying to attract her daughter's attention. Her daughter and her husband had a two-year old child. They were desperate to move house, away from the disturbance that the spirit was causing them each night. After a couple of hours sleep they would be awakened by strange noises downstairs in the living room. Every time they investigated this, they were amazed to see all their child's toys out of the cupboard where they were kept overnight. The daughter and husband told me they were frightened as both watched a toy motor car moving about the living room by itself, also a large plastic ball would be bounced all over the room. Further, writing would appear on a mirror that hung above the fireplace. The words inscribed on it read: 'Please keep the baby.' Every day they scrubbed the writing off the mirror, but the same words would reappear. Finally, they placed it in an outside shed. But that made no difference, the writing continued to come back.

They had no idea who, or what, was causing these problems. The mirror was brought in for me to look at and examine, and I sat down holding it on my knees. Within a few minutes a face started to appear in the mirror, superimposed over my reflection. I described the face of the spirit to them. It was a woman I could see, with short grey hair. Her face was thin and lined with age or worry.

I asked her if she was responsible for moving the toys around and for the writing on the mirror. "Yes", she replied, "I am worried about my daughter's intentions to abort another baby." I asked the lady her name, she answered 'Ethel', and continued to give me more personal information in relation to her time on earth.

After the contact with Ethel, using discretion, I relayed to her daughter the conversation I had received from her mother. Confirming this was accurate, she told me she had aborted one child and was thinking of doing the same again as she was only in the early stages of pregnancy.

One year later I received a letter from the girl, thanking me for the visit. In her letter she told me she now had a healthy baby girl. The disturbances had ceased a week after I had been to her house.

In this particular case Ethel was using these means of disruption to indicate she was worried and angry at her daughter's thoughts of another abortion.

As an intermediary I had been able to give peace of mind to both people.

CHAPTER 11

We sold the house that had been our home for the last ten years. We found it too large and uneconomical for just the two of us. The children having finished university had moved away from Cornwall, each having their respective employment.

I found a cottage for sale on the outskirts of St Austell, it had been used previously as a holiday let. The cottage was constructed of granite, and had apparently been built about two hundred years ago. The rooms inside were quite spacious, and apart from redecoration and installing central heating no other major work would be required. Attached to the cottage was nearly a quarter acre of ground, completely overgrown with brambles and weeds. No problem for me as I love gardening. There was also a large granite built barn, which I presumed could have been in use as a stable many years ago. Just the other side of the waist-high boundary wall was a fast-flowing river that would eventually feed into the sea.

I had a strange feeling that this cottage and its grounds were perhaps predestined in furthering my psychic research. Previous recipients had asked for my new address and telephone number and came back for readings twice a year, and although I had never advertised I was constantly receiving phone calls for readings. No charge was made for the readings, but if they wished they could make a small donation to the two charities of my choice.

I now started to evaluate the accuracy of readings, and I felt satisfied insofar that every reading had been verified. It was becoming quite obvious that the information given to me must be coming from an unknown higher intelligence. I now accepted that the first part of the puzzle had fitted into place and was correct. But being a logical person I was still not satisfied that there was enough definite evidence of immortality. The subject had to be investigated and analysed more thoroughly until I could substantiate irrefutable proof.

Reflecting further on my hypothesis I remembered my precursory experiences in Hertfordshire and knew they could not be disregarded as imagination or illusory, as these etheric people seemed to have the solidity of a normal physical body. Their speech was audible and intelligent, and around them I could sense the vital force of life.

During our life-time on earth the spirit body resides in our physical form, but when the silver cord is broken the vitality or energy force leaves the inanimate earthly body, which can no longer function. This vital energy has then transferred into the perfect spirit duplicate.

The duplicate body can leave the physical body during sleep state, or when a person is under anaesthetic. This is generally known as an 'out of body experience.' Many people have given accurate and detailed descriptions of what they have seen and heard whilst away from their earth body. Such astral travelling is usually involuntary, and safe as long as the silver cord is till attached to the physical body. But a sudden shock of any kind can sever the cord, the result of which would be earthly death.

One of the most interesting facts of astral travelling is that the duplicate body has been seen by other people and later confirmed. An authentic case of such was told to me by a gentleman a few years ago. He frequently experienced projection. On one occasion he found himself floating over open farmland. It was daybreak, but light enough for him to see two men on bicycles and he presumed they were farm labourers on their way to work. He called down to them 'Good morning!' They looked up at him and then quickly threw their bicycles to the ground and cowered down in a ditch at the side of the field.

Later, when he awoke in bed, he remembered the experience and thought it was just a dream. But later the same evening he went down to his local pub for a drink. Unintentionally, he overheard a conversation between a group of men. He was surprised to hear them talk about a man they had seen that morning floating close overhead.

Another classic case of astral projection was told to me by a middle-aged lady whose integrity I have never doubted. She was in hospital for an operation on her stomach, and during the operation she was mentally aware she was close to the ceiling, looking down at her physical body. During the time she was being operated on she heard the conversation between the surgeon and medical staff in attendance. Later the next day she described to the ward-sister exactly what she had seen, and repeated the conversation she had heard between them.

There are numerous accounts of astral travelling that have been witnessed. So what other explanation can be given for this phenomenon, other than we do have a duplicate body. If we do then accept the reality of the spiritual body we have to concede they remain corporeal beings that have previously left the earth plane, because we are aware they still have an active and intelligent brain and mind. Therefore their mental capacity would be, and is, receptive, not only to our thoughts but also our deeds and life style, as they still continue to use every faculty they had on earth.

I started to speculate that my theory had become more constructive than hypothetical. Again I evaluated the knowledge and proof I had obtained over the years. The readings I had given furnished proof and intelligence of the etheric people, accounting for the numerous mortals that have witnessed and experienced phenomena of astral travelling. It had to be more than a possibility that all of us humans do have this duplicate body.

Substantial evidence has been given that the etheric beings not only retain their memory of earth but also have the potentiality of speech and audibility. Now one of the most important pieces in my jigsaw puzzle had fitted into place, and the picture was forming into a pattern. So why did I have this feeling of ambiguity, and what more proof did I need to finally convince myself of immortality? I could find no answers to the latter thoughts. But unbeknown to me, I was very shortly to be given the most ultimate and indisputable proof I could ever imagine.

Six months had passed and we were settled in the cottage. I decided to study for a teaching course on floristry, having previously years ago qualified for the diploma certificate at the Constance Spry College in London. Various teaching courses were to be held throughout the winter months in a large manor house. Years ago it had been a gentleman's private residence, and it was now used as a centre for school inspectors and advisors of higher education. The manor house was within easy walking distance from my cottage and stood in three acres of grounds. A lengthy driveway led to the main entrance. On either side of the front door were two stone pedestals, each with a lifelike stone lion. This imposing entrance opened through to a small vestibule with coat stands and toilet. A large curved stairway was dominent in the main reception hall. Three of the large rooms leading off from the hall were used for lectures and teaching courses, each room with a high ceiling and an ornamental cornice of grape vines and cherubs, reflecting an opulent life style in a bygone age.

By the end of the first month my teaching course was going well. One evening after my course the Chief Inspector asked me whether I would like a few hours employment at the house that would not affect the course I was on. The job would entail being a key holder, answering any telephone enquiries and logging out any computers that the office staff had left on. I accepted the post as it was close to home, also the monthly salary would be useful. And so I found myself the keeper of this beautiful house, and its security.

The first strange experience occurred one morning at seven thirty. It was an early start to the day but I had to be there to unlock the door and take the alarm off. The lady cleaner was sitting in her car. She told me she had arrived at twenty past seven and waited by the front door for me to arrive. "I think", she said, "you had better call the police, there is someone inside the house." I asked why she suspected that, and she told me she had heard someone laughing and talking just behind the locked door. She was really nervous, so I knew she was not joking with me.

I told her to stay close behind me as I unlocked the door, tapping the security code in to stop the alarm, I then re-bolted the door. Taking a large rolled umbrella from the coat stand we proceeded to search the whole of the house. We found nothing untoward to indicate a human presence in the house.

I had never mentioned spirit phenomena to her, but two months later she resigned from her job. She told me she always felt she was being watched by someone invisible.

A new lady cleaner was now employed at the house. She had no previous knowledge of the house being haunted, and I had no intention of enlightening her on its unseen inhabitants. However, she did occasionally complain of an intense coldness around her. I could not give her any satisfactory answer to this. It was mid September and the evenings were dark by five-thirty. A series of inexplicable events started to happen. Several times in one week I was awakened by the police phoning me as the alarm system had gone off, and I was requested to meet the police over at the house. Two police cars were outside the main door as my husband and I arrived. I went through the procedure of resetting the alarm and accompanied by the police searched all rooms. But no forced entry had been made. The alarm system was thoroughly checked but no fault with it was found.

The next incident nearly gave me a heart attack. Unlocking the main door one morning I walked straight into the medical skeleton. It had been placed immediately behind the door. After tapping in the alarm code I picked up 'Mr Bones' as I called him, and carried him down the long corridor back to the resources room where he was kept. As I was the only key holder to the house, no one else could have entered to play this joke on me. There was only one answer to the mystery, and I knew for certain it was no physical being.

Numerous incidents kept occurring over the next few months, but my patience came to an end when a dozen or more sheets of white copier paper came floating down from the upstairs bannisters and lay scattered on the hall carpet. At the time I was alone in the house. Slowly, I picked up the papers, looked up at the bannisters and said out loud: "Alright you s...s. You're not frightening me with your jokes. If you think you are so clever materialise yourself, so we can all see you!"

I did not think for one moment they would take me seriously, but two days later, picking up the morning post, I heard somebody walking down the stairs. I stared in amazement at a tall elegant lady wearing an evening gown. She smiled at me, and said "Good morning." I had barely answered her when she became semi diaphanous. Three seconds later, as I watched she vanished.

The appearance of materialised spirits began to escalate, not only for me but the staff as well. I was secretly pleased at this, as it only confirmed it was not my imagination. The lady cleaner threatened to leave, as she had several times seen a semi-transparent young boy dressed in old-fashioned clothes. Also, a gentleman was seen by myself and several members of staff. He always seemed physically solid, and was usually seen limping along the corridor upstairs. Obviously, he had at some time while on the earth plane damaged his left leg.

One of the Head Advisers asked me one day who was the man limping along the corridor. I had to answer his questions with ambiguity as I had no knowledge of the spirit gentleman's name. I just presumed he was the previous owner of the house. The Head Adviser looked at me quizzically. "Well", he said, "dam funny. When he's walking in front of me, goes into the copier room. I follow him in, and the room seems empty. Do you think we have ghosts?" I smiled at him and replied: "More than likely".

These spirit inhabitants of the house were intelligent, and knew exactly what the house was being used for and everybody that used it. I realised after a few more months that their annoying jokes had finished. They were still around in the house, and were seen several times a week by myself and most of the staff. We accepted them, as we knew they meant us no harm.

These spirits were not ghosts of the past, they were living entities that were earth-bound, because they had no desire to leave the surroundings they had been used to. Perhaps one day they would evolve to a higher plane and leave their past life behind.

It may seem preposterous to many people that the spirit people can also use their energy to manipulate machinery and instruments, including the telephone. I experienced the latter, one Saturday afternoon in the summer. I had opened up the house at nine-thirty a.m., as a lecture for students was to be given at ten-thirty, until two p.m. My husband and myself walked over at one forty-five. We watched everyone leave including the lecturer. Checking all rooms, we found the window in the lecture room had been opened but there was no key to lock it. My husband suggested we just push the catch over, he thought it would be secure enough. But I worried about it, and we spent three quarters of an hour looking everywhere for the key. It could not be found.

We had only been back home for ten minutes when the phone rang. I answered it, giving our number, and a gentleman's cultured voice said: "The key you are looking for is on the coffee table in the lecture room." I asked to whom I was speaking but the line went dead. I quickly did a recall 1471, and the operator gave me the number and the time of call from the house. "Quick", I said to my husband, "someone has rung from the house." We practically ran all the way over to the house, unlocked the door, disengaged the alarm and found the key as stated on the coffee table.

Later in the evening I phoned the lecturer at his home, asking if he had telephoned me earlier about the lost key. "No", he replied. "I'm sorry, I should have phoned and told you I couldn't find the key to re-lock the window."

Maybe it was fortuitous when I met an old lady whilst shopping. She had previously lived in our neighbourhood and was now in her eighties. During our conversation she asked me if I was employed. She was surprised when I told her where I worked. "I know that house very well", she said. "It was my first job when I left school at fourteen. I was employed there as a housemaid. It was hard work, having to be up every morning at four-thirty, clean out and relight all the fires, and heat water for the gentry's baths. They used to entertain a lot in those days, you know, always had visitors staying in the house." She paused for breath, so I took the opportunity to ask her whether she remembered a tall elegant lady who lived there or visited the house. "Oh yes!" she replied, "that was the Countess of Athlone. She was always polite to us girls."

Before I could ask her more questions she told me about her employer. "Very strict he was, liked everything in order. He was a Colonel in the army at one time, and he would buy anything that was in fashion. One day he buys this brand-new motor bike, has a bad crash and smashed up his left leg. He recovered from the accident, but it always left him with a bad limp. They were a wealthy family but didn't have much luck. Their only son died from a bad illness when he was five years old."

After listening to the old lady's history of the house and its previous owners one could only guess at the tragedy and sadness that must have existed at that time. Perhaps the constant stream of visitors and lavish entertainment helped in some way to alleviate their darker days.

Having firsthand confirmation of these former inhabitants of the house was gratifying in the sense that all the staff and I had not been under some illusion or prey to imagination. The continuity of manifestations led to regular appearances inside and outside the house. The local people walking their dogs at night became aware of these supernatural happenings and consequently avoided the grounds surrounding the house.

During the subsequent years of my employment substantial proof of an afterlife was given to many people. There was so much in the way of psychic phenomena occurring and being witnessed that it would take much time to record. We became accustomed to the spirit people and never sensed any malevolence from them, just curiosity. After all, we were strangers in their home.

I was rather amused one day when a lecturer on Judaism came to speak with me. He told me he thought he had seen the gentleman with the limp walking down the stairs. He gave an accurate description of the spirit. I asked him: "Do you think it was only your imagination?" He thought for a moment. "No", he replied, "too solid for that. I think it's possibly a defect with the optic nerve of the eye."

"Would you be of the same opinion", I said, "if I told you many members of the staff and myself have witnessed this same gentleman collectively?" He looked nonplused for a while. "I can give no logical answer to that", he replied, "it's beyond my comprehension."

We are consciously aware of what we see and sense around us in our world. And when we are fully awake there are differences in alertness during these hours. These changes of alertness are of two types, and are mediated by different systems within the brain.

Firstly, there are tonic differences which reflect intrinsic slow changes of the basal level of arousal of our everyday thoughts and thinking.

Secondly, there is a phasic change of alertness which reflects a short-lived variation in an organism's arousal over a period of seconds, and which is initiated by unusual or important events. During these phasic changes when we are preoccupied with our everyday thoughts and work, we can be unaware of the heightened arousal of our psychic senses. Consequently, when any form of genuine psychic phenomena manifests we visualise it with reality and not the thinking or imaginative part of our brain.

Imagination works in close conjunction with the tonic differences in the brain, and we use this ability to create in either a practical way, or to prompt thoughts of happiness or fear, etc. Again, we are using the thought process, which also of course can, with any form of suggestion or stimuli, prompt one to think they have seen or heard something of a supernatural source.

I remember a true story told to me by a gentleman a few years ago that gives an excellent example of the phasic change within the brain. He had arrived early at the house for the evening class, and asked me if he could make himself a coffee. He followed me through to the kitchen, remarking on the elegant interior of the house. After conversing for a few minutes he suddenly asked me: "Is this house haunted?"

I was hesitant in replying, and then said some people had sensed and seen odd things at times. "Why do you ask?" I said. Putting his empty cup and saucer in the sink he replied: "I sensed a strange feeling of someone watching me in the hallway." I smiled. "Do you believe in spirits?" I asked. "Well, I had never been interested or believed in ghosts, spirits, or whatever people call them, until two years ago." He went on to relate his strange story to me.

"My wife and I had been to Plymouth for the day, shopping spree you know. We were driving home to Redruth, where we live. It was a fine evening, still quite light, and we were nearly into Camborne when we saw a young lady standing by the side of the road. She raised one arm to motion us to stop. I stopped the car and unwound the window. 'What's up love' I asked, 'you need help?' She nodded, and then said to us: 'Lift please to number ten Rose Hill Crescent, Camborne.' 'Certainly', I said, 'hang on. You have to get in this way to sit in the back.' I pulled my driving seat forward, and she climbed in.

"She never spoke to us to explain why she needed the lift, and my wife turned round and asked her again for the address she needed. The young girl repeated it again and we drove on in silence.

"It wasn't long before we found the Crescent and pulled up outside number ten. 'Here you are', I said. 'I'll have to pull my seat forward again to let you out.' But there was no answer. My wife and I looked around, and there was no-one in the back of the car." He paused for a moment and I asked him:"Where did she go?" "You tell me", he said. "It was not possible for her to get out of the car until the front seat was pulled forward."

Continuing with his story he said: "Well, you can imagine how we felt. Were we dreaming this?" I asked my wife, but of course it was no dream. We sat there for five or six minutes discussing this uncanny incident. Finally I said to my wife: "I'm going to knock at that door number ten, and as we have a good description of the girl find out why she asked for this address". We knocked hard at number ten, and after a few moments a grey haired lady opened the door. I explained we had given a lift to a young girl who had asked for her address. I had started to give a description of the girl when the lady quietly said. "Thank you. I am sorry you have been troubled, she keeps on doing this". Before I could ask her to explain she started to close the door, saying: "Thank you. Please forget about it". Well, we couldn't forget about it. we walked back back to the car, puzzled and disturbed. The girl had looked as solid as my wife and I.

Driving back the way we had come there was no sign of the girl again. I remembered earlier we had passed a police station. "I'm going in", I said. "Maybe they can tell us something. They will think you're mad" my wife replied. "I spoke to a youngish police officer at the desk." "Did you knock her down, mate?" he asked. "No," I sighed. "I just told you what happened, and I'm not going crazy." "Hold on a minute, I'll get the sergeant." After a couple of minutes a plump sergeant comes from the back, eating a packet of crisps. "Right" he said. "Tell me what happened." I went through the story again. "Number ten Rose Hill Crescent, you say?" Feeling stupid, I almost whispered "Yes." "Oh yea," he replied, "we know all about that. That girl was run over two years ago or more on that piece of road. Killed outright I believe. You're not the first one to call here. We've had scores of people come in and tell us they've given her a lift to that address, and she disappears before they even stop. She just haunts that piece of road. Shame really for her parents."

"We took an alternative route back home", the gentleman said, "but the wife and I will never forget that girl." I thanked him for telling me the story and I sensed he was honest and serious.

CHAPTER 12

Beyond the threshold of our earth plane exist the etheric worlds, invisible to our eyes but a reality to the Spirit inhabitants that have previously lived on earth. Altogether, there are seven dimensions including our world. And with the continuous development of a higher spirituality the etherians or spirit people will gradually ascend through every dimension until they have reached a state of perfection - the purity of spirit. The many that cannot or have no wish to continue to the next dimension can choose to return to the earth plane. This is known as reincarnation. And so the physical and spiritual life force continues in cycles.

Our physical body disintegrates when we die, and if a human physical body when expired is dissected the etheric body with some of its components would not be found. The mind, soul and memory cannot perish. As they are not of a physical substance they will continue their use within the etheric body. The existence of the etheric body has been proved over aeons with authentic communications from the so-called dead.

Scientists are concerned with what they can see or experiment on. They also live and work with facts, whereas psychics work and live with unseen matter, and psychic energy goes beyond any scientific studies.

At the time of writing I noticed a television programme in which it was stated that scientists are considering the creation of a human head and body from a collection of cells, blood etc. in the laboratory. It will always be impossible to create a complete human being in this way, as the most important component would be absent: the spirit or soul that enters the brain of the embryo after about three months of gestation.

Paranormal experiences are inconsistent with physical theories, although some paranormal phenomena may become explicable when new physical discoveries are made. A very few scientists in the early 1950s did try experiments with different mediums. In 1953 a well-known biologist, Sir Alister Hardy of Oxford University, gave reasons why his scientific colleagues would not accept psychic work, mainly because, I believe, the psychic experiments could not be repeated in a laboratory. Personally, I do not think this is a satisfying answer. As we know, psychic phenomena cannot be produced on demand or just to satisfy curiosity. The conditions in a laboratory would not create the harmonious atmosphere needed for psychic phenomena. The other consisted of - a waste of time and/or it was impossible.

I regard all genuine psychic work more as a science as amongst other things it embraces the dormant senses within ourselves, and also we begin to understand and gain knowledge of the energies of earth, biology and the cosmic. Spiritualism presents its own proof, without having to believe in it.

I personally do not classify Spiritualism as a religion. To me it is a natural way of life that brings knowledge and enlightenment of immortality. The human tendency to want to believe in life after death makes objective appraisal of the evidence peculiarly difficult, but some psychic researchers maintain that communications coming through genuine mediums point clearly to human survival.

There are many mysteries to life and death that are still inexplicable to us, and perhaps we shall never learn, or understand the answers that remain in our minds.

One of the mysteries is the theory of reincarnation. There have been many very evidential case histories of earlier incarnations where people have recalled past lives, or deja vu. These memories of a former life, or lives, come from the subconscious mind, and with most of these authentic cases they cannot possibly be classed as imagination. The most probable explanation would seem to be reincarnation.

I recall a friend of mine telling me she had always had an overpowering feeling she had to visit Greece. This feeling had been with her for years, but unfortunately her husband and herself could never afford to travel there until they both retired from work. With some of their retirement money they booked a holiday in Greece. They had never been there before, and it was a completely new environment for them.

On the second night of their holiday. Fiona had a dream, where she was walking down small alleyways until she came to a house she felt familiar with. An old man came out of the house and started talking to her in Greek, and she replied to him in the same language. When she woke up her husband told her she had been talking in her sleep. "It sounded like some foreign language," he said.

A few days later they bought tickets for a day tour in the surrounding countryside, stopping several times to visit places of interest. At midday they arrived at a small village for lunch, with the afternoon free to explore until five o'clock. "I felt as if I had been here before", she said, "and started walking fast down small alleyways. My husband said to me: "What's the hurry, we've got plenty of time". "I know this place, I must find my house", I replied.

"Well, I did find my house, and I just stood there looking at it. It was so familiar to me I cried. And then the strangest thing happened. An old man with white hair came out of the open doorway. He kept staring at me, and spoke to me in Greek. I answered him in his own language. He told me I resembled his daughter who had died many years ago. I felt an affinity with him as if I had known him before in a past life."

Fiona has been a friend of mine for many years and I have never had reason to doubt her story. The only language she speaks is English, and a little French.

Amongst other strange things that may account for reincarnation is that many people over the years have displayed skills that normally require a lifetime of training. Also children, at a very early age, have shown unusual talent and understanding of difficult music. One of these child prodigies was Wolfgang Amadeus Mozart, who composed music at the age of four.

For centuries there have been similar cases of a remembrance of a past life, when people have recalled being fatally injured by accident or design, and still bear marks on their body that resemble the scars of acquired wounds, also strange birthmarks that cannot always be explained by genetics. It makes us wonder sometimes whether a disastrous accident or event in a past life can account for an existing emotional disturbance in some people: fear of fire, water, or perhaps travel, that can be retained in the latent memory.

Many religions throughout the world have embraced belief in reincarnation. The Holy Bible in some of its chapters gives accounts of afterlife and reincarnation. These spiritual theories are not a New Age idea, they have been understood and recognised by ancient civilisations of centuries ago.

I felt pressed to write the following account of a reincarnation that occurred only a few years ago in Dorset, England.

A young woman had lost her first and only child, a boy aged six. He had wandered from home, across fields and onto a railway line, and was killed by an oncoming train. After a year the bereaved parents moved house two miles away from where they had previously lived. Eighteen months later the young woman gave birth to another son, whom she named Robert. When Robert reached school age his mother always escorted him to and from school. He asked her: "Why can't I walk home by myself like the other boys do?" She told him there was too much traffic on the road, and she would be worried about him crossing by himself.

"There is always someone", he said, "who would help me to cross the road, not like the railway line where I was run over by a train." She looked at him in amazement. "When did a train run you over?" she asked. "Oh, a long time ago", he answered, "but I do remember where it happened."

Later in the evening she repeated Robert's story to her husband. "Well", he said, "he could not have known about the child being run over. It was several years ago now and we are comparatively strangers in this new district. Anyway, don't you remember, Dr Beeching had closed that particular line and many more like it." But they were still puzzled by the child's story.

About a month later, on a Sunday, they went for a drive in the car and parked half a mile away from the old disused rail track. "Come on Robert", said Father, "we are going to stretch our legs for a while and take a small walk in the fresh air." They crossed a couple of fields and stopped to pick a few wild flowers. Suddenly, Robert stared a short way ahead of them. "Let's go down the sloping path I know", he said. "I can't see a path", his father said, "show us". Robert ran ahead of them and pointed to a patch of overgrown ferns. "The pathway is in here", he said. Brushing the ferns to one side they followed the path down a slight slope. Reaching the end of the slope, they could just see the old rail line. Nature had taken over and it was overgrown with self-set wild flowers and bushes. Robert's parents knew the line had been there, but Robert had no present knowledge of it. Robert said quietly: "That's where I was run over by the train, but I only remember a lot of people around, and I could see myself being carried away from the rail."

Your guess is as good as mine. Could he, a child of six, invent this story?

There is much evidence of rebirth from all over the world, but not all souls that are reborn always come back to their original parents, or location. And if reincarnation is a positive fact, the big question is "Why are souls reborn?"

Many suggestions have been put forward that our lives are a continuous circle which we all have to experience until we are spiritually perfect, and then eventually we can ascend to the highest dimension, the Godhead, our Creator. Other answers to this question have been given, to the effect that we have the opportunity to learn from our mistakes and faults when on earth, or to experience pain and hardship that we had not encountered in a previous life. Perhaps we shall never know the correct reason if, or why, we re-enter this earth plane, and I personally do not think it is a problem to be concerned about at present.

To conclude this topic of reincarnation I quote a writing of the German philosopher Immanuel Kant, born in 1724:

"In view of the endless duration of the immortal soul throughout the infinity of time, shall the soul remain for ever attached to this point of world space on earth, will it never participate in a closer contemplation of the remaining wonders of creation? Who knows, but that the intention is for it to become acquainted at close range some day with these far distant globes of the cosmic system, which from this distance already provoke our curiosity."

Over the last fifty years I have given numerous psychic readings to people from all walks of life. For each recipient the readings would cover their past, present and the future, but these readings are not fortune telling.

During the readings I would see clairvoyantly, and hear the spirit people audibly that had gathered around the recipient to prove their continued existence in another dimension. On occasions, the recipients would bring me an object to hold in my hands. This is called Psychometry. I would be able to feel and sense the vibrations and emanations that would effuse from the object. This is a very interesting aspect of psychic work as sometimes an object, whatever it may be, can give off these emanations relating to the present, or to past centuries.

One of the most interesting accounts of an object holding vibrations and emanations was told to me one day, after I had given a gentleman a personal reading. He lived and worked in London, and had come to Cornwall with his wife for a week's holiday. I shall relate his story as I think it is worth mention. But firstly I will transcribe a small part of the reading I gave him concerning an old urn that was still holding strong but evil emanations.

"I can see you now on a wide river in a long narrow boat, but you are not fishing. All sorts of things are being pulled up from the river into the boat, mostly debris I would say." "Yes", he replied, "I know what you mean".

"There is a man helping you, and I will describe him to you. He has not passed over into spirit, he works with you. This man never seems to stop talking to you, and he is wearing a hat that looks like a battered old straw boater with several wine corks hanging all around the rim. I can't take my eyes off this character", I said. The gentleman rocked with laughter in his chair. "I know him", he said, "I'll you all about him after the reading."

I was intrigued by the next thing I could see clairvoyantly. My sitter was holding up a large urn that he had hauled up from out of the water. It looked to me as if it was silver, but badly tarnished. "What I can't understand", I said, "is why I'm seeing, of all things, bats flying around this large urn." "Yes", he replied, "I most certainly know what you are telling me. I will explain it later." The reading went on with quite a few more interesting facts I saw for him.

When the hour's reading was finished he told me his story. He and his mate I had described were dredgers on the Thames in London. During one of these dredging sessions six months ago he had dredged up from the depths of the Thames this large urn. "I'm taking this home", he told his mate. "I'll clean it up. If it's silver it could be worth a lot of money."

"Well", he said, "I gave it a bit of a clean up, and from what I had cleaned I could see it was good solid silver, and it was empty inside. I told my wife: 'I'll finish cleaning it tomorrow, but for tonight I'll put it on the bathroom windowsill', which I did, and closed the window and the door.

Later on I was undressing, ready for bed, and my wife went to the bathroom. Suddenly I heard her scream. I thought she had been taken ill, so I rushed in to her. My wife had her hands over her head, terrified, and flying around our small bathroom were five or six bats".

Pausing for a moment in his story, I could see he was still reliving the horror of that night. Continuing his story he said: "I pushed my wife out of the bathroom, opened the window and grabbed a towel. Finally I got all the bats out of the window, and even threw the towel out as well. I searched the bathroom until I was satisfied there were no more, closed the window and door, and went to bed.

"Next morning being Saturday, the wife and I had a bit of a lie in bed. But, you're not going to believe this. I swear to God it's true. I was the first one to use the bathroom, and as I opened the door there were were several bats flying around the room again. I managed to get them out of the window, but I had a feeling of something evil in connection with the old urn.

"I carried the urn downstairs, put it in a cardboard box and later in the morning took it to the National Museum. The curator who examined it told me it was solid silver and very old, dating back a couple of centuries or more. I never mentioned the bats, just told him I had dredged it up from the Thames. The Curator told me the vase was valuable, and had probably been used for black witchcraft rituals in the past. He went to hand it back to me, but I said: 'No, you keep it for the museum.'"

Although my gentleman sitter had sensed evil from the urn, had he acquired the faculty of clairvoyance it would have enabled him to gain more information regarding the urn.

Psychometry practised by a genuine medium can be of great value in helping the police in their investigations of a murder or other crime. An object or an article of clothing left at the scene of the crime will be held in the hands of the medium. The emanations that effuse from whatever is held can usually give a good description and more information about the culprit responsible.

Articles of clothing or jewellery that are sometimes given to a relative or friend of a deceased person can also send emanations to the new owner, not always found to be of a pleasant nature. If the deceased person had suffered from a chronic illness, or even depression, the symptoms of the illness can be transmitted to the present owner.

I know a gentleman who was given a watch by a lady. Her husband had died five years previously and she had kept his watch in a drawer. The watch was in good condition, and when a new battery was fitted kept perfect time. The gentleman in question had no previous knowledge of the owner of the watch, nor the reason for his death. After wearing the watch for a week he started to experience bad pains in his chest. His doctor could not find anything wrong with his chest, and an E.C.G. proved his heart was normal. The pains ceased when he removed the watch at bedtime. Eventually he took the watch off completely. When he made discreet enquiries to the widow about her late husband's health when he was on the earth plane, she told him her husband had suffered from a heart problem for some years. His death was due to a fatal heart attack.

Part of the mystic subconscious can filter into our dreams and premonitions. Most people dream at some time when asleep, some of course more that others. Dreams can quite often be the aftermath of eating too much late at night, or if our mind has been troubled or worried by some news, or event that has occurred recently, or even way back in the past. Carl Jung, the Swiss psychologist, told of his belief in the existence of a collective unconscious, derived from ancestral experiences. Are we then, in respect of what he said, drawing from our subconscious when asleep and bringing forward into another part of the mind pictures of the past, or future?

Dreams fall into different categories, and what are known as the 'in depth' dreams are mainly clairvoyance and premonitory. The latter are usually shown as something foreboding about to happen, but not always in our own life. Of course clairvoyance and premonitions can also occur during our daytime hours, as both these faculties stem from the subconscious part of the brain, although we are unaware of it being used.

Both dreams and premonitions can be in colour, which is really only highlighting the importance of a forthcoming situation or event. So if these prophetic dreams and premonitions later prove to be a reality, it seems reasonable to consider influences outside our own mind.

I recall a very disturbing premonition and clairvoyant dream I had in August 1997, regarding Her Royal Highness, Princess Diana. While watching the television news one evening, close-up pictures of Princess Diana and Dodi, Mr Al Fayed's son, were being shown. They both looked happy, and yet a little strain was showing on their faces as they were probably aware that the world was waiting to hear an announcement of marriage between them. As I watched them I had an awful premonition that they were going to die very soon. "That cannot be correct," I thought, "maybe I'm just tired."

Later that same night I awoke from what I presumed had been a nightmare. I had been in an underground tunnel and I saw a car had crashed into a concrete pillar. As I drew closer to the car, I could see human bodies lying still. Early next morning the dreadful news was given out on television and radio that Diana, Princess of Wales, had met with a tragic accident that had caused her death.

There have been numerous accounts of people who have reported tragic disasters and accidents before they occurred, but premonitions are only of interest if given before the actual event occurs. One of such was the terrible disaster that happened one Friday morning in October 1966. A mass of coal waste was loosened by torrential rain, and slid down a valley enveloping the Panglas Junior School in Aberfan, Wales. A little girl of nine had told her mother the day before she had dreamt of a big black mass covering her school. Tragically, she was one of the many children who died in that event.

But many vivid accounts of this tragedy were foretold before it happened. One lady living two hundred miles away had a premonition of the Aberfan disaster thirty minutes before the school was demolished by the coal waste. The accuracy and descriptions were so convincing it left no doubt as to the fact that many people have the potential of premonition.

With every serious investigation of psychic dreams and premonitions a clue emerges to the mystery of why and how so many people at times can foresee important events. If we accept Carl Jung's hypothesis that the answer is to be found in the collective subconscious, the only logical answer has to be that people are receptive when they are not actually thinking, i.e. when asleep or completely relaxed. It is during these times that the Alpha rhythms function with the Phasic within the nonconscious part of the brain or mind.

The Yogi, by meditating on the Ajna chakra which has a connection with the pineal gland, can gain psychic powers. But for people who do not meditate the same semi-conscious state can be acquired naturally when they are in a passive or quiet frame of mind, without realising the same channels are opened and receptive to precognition and clairvoyance during day-time, and sleep state.

CHAPTER 13

Over the years, people have mentioned spiritual healing to me and the same question is asked: "Do you have to have faith in it to work?" I answer this question with ambivalence because people can react differently to the various techniques that are sometimes used with spiritual healing. Personally, I do not think faith is essential, although I admit the power of suggestion can be useful, and helpful in calming the mind and body of a sick person. The mind, again, plays an important part in healing. Medical practitioners are well aware of this fact when on occasion they administer a placebo to a patient. As fear can create poisons within the body, passive thoughts can help the healing capacities to regulate the flow of vitality within the body.

There is an invisible flow of magnetic current through all objects, including the human body. This indefinable force, sometimes called the vital force, is dependent on harmony within and outside the body. During contact healing a genuine healer will radiate a sense of empathy while working on the patient.

Most healers lightly touch or place their hands directly onto the afflicted parts. There are also good healers who can transmit the energy force by holding their hands two or three inches above the patient. This invisible energy forms a vapour pattern from the healer to the sick person, and this vapour pattern can be seen visually if a glass of cold water is held by the healer directly after the healing.

Another technique of healing is 'biofeedback'. However, this requires mental help from the patient, and for the many people who have experienced the efficacy of visualisation the results of such can be beneficial and rewarding. During 'biofeedback' a patient may be connected to a sensitive monitor that will record what is happening within their body. The patient is asked to visualise and concentrate on that part which is causing the problem. If, for instance, the illness is of a terminal nature the healer may suggest to the patient that he or she visualise the offending disease being blasted by crystal particles that would help to eradicate it and cleanse the diseased area. Biofeedback is similar to self-hypnosis, as both methods are using the mind to control the body. With all these forms of healing it has been found that there were significant changes in the haemoglobin that carries oxygen to the tissues and the vital force within the body.

Increased control over the body by the mind has been observed and used over decades by Yogis and many Eastern religions. Their awareness of the vital force was called by different names. The Egyptians named it the Ka, the Hindus Prana, and the Chinese use the word Chi. All spiritual healing can be therapeutic, and all diseases and disabilities can be helped, or curative if treated at an early stage. A sick person can be instrumental in helping mentally to influence the healing process with visualisation. The onus of course depends much on the will-power of the patient to help overcome the ailment.

So are credence and faith required for spiritual healing? The answer is definitely no. Absent healing can be very effective, and curative in many forms of illness. This is extraordinary in respect to the fact that no form of participation is required from the patient. Harry Edwards, founder of the National Federation of Spiritual Healers in England, objected to the term 'faith healing' because it implied that faith was essential for a person to be cured. He knew from his experience of healing many people that it was untrue. Long distances between healer and patient make no difference to the healing process. Healer and patient can be physically unknown to each other, and usually no information regarding the patient is needed other than the Christian name and the nature of the illness. The thought force from the healer is a current of energy as real as a current of air or electricity. If the illness is incipient, the healing process can be quicker to respond.

Another famous healer was Edgar Cayce who practised absent healing for forty-three years. During a trance state he would make a diagnosis of a person's illness and then suggest a treatment for the patient, mainly of various herbs or manipulation of the body. It was thought that while in trance he was controlled by a spirit doctor, as he had no previous knowledge of conventional medicine, but his cures of various diseases were remarkable.

The absence of faith or credence in paranormal healing proves its worth especially when contact, or absent, healing is given to children or animals as they are completely unaware of any unusual outside influence from spirit. These energies that are generated from the healer's mind or hands are without doubt a factor in restoring health. I have seen and heard of many instances of absent healing on children and animals. Years ago, when I lived in Hertfordshire, I owned a Labrador dog and unfortunately he developed a large tumour in the large intestine. The veterinary surgeon I took him to told me it was inoperable and suggested putting him to sleep. I contacted a well-known healer in London, a Mr Gordon Turner, and took my dog to him for healing, travelling by car. After making two visits to Mr Turner he told me he would continue by absent healing.

To be honest there was not much hope for the dog's recovery as he was old, but after two weeks there was a vast improvement in his condition, the life force within him seemed to be regenerated. A month later I revisited the veterinary surgeon. After a careful examination and X-rays it was found that the tumour had gone. My dog continued to live for another healthy five years.

Crystals are used by some healers, either by placing them on parts of the patient's body or holding the crystal over the affected part. The prismatic colours are the same as the spectrum in the rainbow. Atomic patterns are contained within them and they give off vibrations that may be beneficial for the patient. Colour is caused by, and responds to, a higher range of vibrations around us. Whether it is the colour or the vibrations that heal we are not sure, possibly a combination of both. But colour is important in our lives and can affect us in different ways. When I give a reading to a person, usually I can see the aura around their head. If the aura is showing blue, white or gold I know the person is in good health. Red shows me anger and frustration. The colours yellow and green depict illness of body or mind.

Even in our daily lives colours can affect our moods by uplifting or depressing us. Most people I think have had the experience, like myself, of changing an article of clothing for another colour, as the harmony between mind and the colour did not feel right on that particular day. The same may apply to any colour we use in our homes.

All healing entails working on a person's or an animal's psyche, as well as the body. Music and colour are quite often used together in healing. We are aware of the fact that in our physical world there are seven major colours, and seven major tones in music. But in the etheric world there is a greater variety of colour and tones of music than we know of. When we look at a rainbow we perceive the seven colours, but further ranges of colour extend on either side of the spectrum. As mortals we cannot see, or respond to, these higher vibrations unless we have an extrasensory gift and of course the same applies to audible sounds.

Many composers of music have been inspired by vibratory activity that comes from the higher spheres of the esoteric world. If you have been fortunate enough to have heard spirit music you will realise that it is superior in every way to our earth music. You may be surprised to learn that each colour corresponds to a tone of music. For instance, the key of C relates to the colour blue. Therefore, music with the chords of C that predominate is mainly used for spiritual development and upliftment. The E of music is used for terminal illness, and liver, the corresponding colours are green and yellow. The tone of B corresponds to the colour violet, used for many parts of the body including the mind. It would take time to transcribe all the different combinations here, but all these different frequencies and sounds can stimulate and regenerate the organs of the body.

All healing by psychic means involves the intangible, but there is still controversy between medical practitioners as to whether it actually works, or whether it is all a question of mind over matter. What difference does it make, if it is curative?

Within a few years from now, I feel, conventional and complementary healing will work closer together and co-exist in hospitals for the benefit of mankind.

My employment in this apparitional house would soon be finished, because I had to take compulsory retirement at sixty five. I was saddened by this as I was still in good health, mentally and physically. I knew I would miss 'the House' and its spirit occupants. They were still consistent in their appearances to myself and most of the staff.

Over the last five years there had been a constant change of employees because of the spirit activity. These spirit entities were not malevolent, but they knew we were still aware of their presence. I think they had accepted us, as we had come to accept them. Also, their teasing had stopped. Many times they would appear as solid as us mortals, and within seconds become semi diaphanous. Exorcism had been suggested by one member of staff, but nobody seemed to be interested in organising one, so nothing was arranged and the subject was finally forgotten. And for my part I was pleased there had been no exorcism, as I knew these spirits were happy in their own environment.

Often I would hear their laughter and speech, so why should they be evicted from their home? It was their choice if they wished to remain close to earth, or to evolve to a higher plane. However, not all spirits that remain close to the earth plane are happy, and one young lady spirit was badly in need of help to adjust to a higher level.

A new caretaker-plus-odd-job man had been recently employed. He had a small workshop adjoined to the rear of 'the House'. Apparently, years ago, it had been used as a chapel. This small room was empty except for the caretaker's workbench, and a couple of chairs. Every afternoon I would knock at his door, and ask if he would like a cup of tea or coffee.

On this particular day I knocked, the door was slightly open but there was no reply. I called again, but no answer. Suddenly, an overpowering scent of flowers emanated from his room. I stood transfixed when clairvoyantly I saw a young girl of medium height with shoulder length fair hair. She looked desperately unhappy, and was wearing a long white gown trimmed with lace. I received the impression it was a nightgown. Her right hand was resting on a closed coffin, the lid of which was covered with flowers of lilies and roses.

I knew immediately she was of the spirit world, but for some reason she was earth-bound. "What is your name?" I asked her. With almost a whisper she answered: "Estelle". Moving closer to her, I said: "How can I help you?" She made no answer, but raised her left hand towards me. I felt an icy coldness from her, and throughout my body an intense sensation of pain. I closed my eyes and prayed for the girl. Within less than five minutes the pain left me.

As I opened my eyes the girl and the coffin with the flowers had gone, and the caretaker's workshop was back to normal. For just a few moments I had taken on these conditions of the young girl's death and released her from the traumatic experience she had endured. One hour later I found the caretaker, working downstairs in the cellar dismantling an old sideboard. "Have you got your workshop organised now as you want it?" I asked. "Just about" he replied, "except the problem is it always feels so damn cold in there, like an ice-box".

I made no mention to him, or anyone else, of what I had seen or experienced.

A month later, before I finally left my employment, I was chatting to one of the groundsmen. He was pruning a few shrubs close to the house. "Pity", I said, "they don't grow a few beds of roses here instead of these shrubs. Pushing his cap back from his forehead, he said: "Used to grow them in the old days when me gran'dad was gardener up here at house. Gran'dad used to tell me the Master had beds of roses, lilies and all sorts, 'cos of course plenty of manure from the stables in those days yer know."

I watched him as he finished pruning the Forsythia shrub. I sensed there was more he had to say, and when he straightened up from his pruning he again took up the story: "Gran'dad told me, Master made him dig up all the roses and lilies when she died." "Who died?" I asked. "His daughter of course. Didn't you know?"

Truthfully I replied: "No, I didn't know".

He hesitated for a moment and then spoke again: "Weren't very old when she had the accident, teenager. Lorry tippled over onto pavement and crushed her. Gran'dad told me Master went a bit funny in 'is head after that. Wouldn't have her buried for two months, kept her in the small chapel there, back of the house."

As an intermediary between the two worlds I had taken on the conditions of this young girl's pains for a few moments, releasing her finally from her mental trauma by acting as a conductor to neutralise her memories of the accident.

During a reading for people I will often be given, and feel, the symptoms of an illness or disability that the spirit person has endured whilst on earth. These symptoms are only ephemeral and are given as evidence to prove their identity, as also their acquired characteristics and mannerisms. These spirit people who communicate through me to the recipient are free of all pain and accept the fact that they have departed from the earth plane.

As we gain more knowledge of immortality the fear of death

decreases. There is more fear in the thought of how, or what illness may cause the cessation of our earthly life, and in some cases we are ourselves responsible for our own health and wellbeing, unless the cause is of a genetic nature.

Life on earth is transitory and rather like a training ground, and the cycle of living and dying is continuous. Belief in this has been recorded by many philosophers. Pythagoras stated, and I quote: "Life on the earth plane is necessary for the development of our soul, although the lessons we learn may be very difficult to bear at times." And most of these ancient philosophers possessed more knowledge and wisdom regarding immortality and reincarnation than the majority of people today.

These same attributes have also to be applied to the primitive and ancient civilisations that once inhabited the earth. It would be inconceivable to think of the ancient people as ignorant, as we know they attained knowledge not only of immortality but of many of the sciences, and the construction of buildings. The faultless structures of the pyramids in Egypt and elsewhere on other continents were built with such precision that it leaves us with no doubt as to the high level of intelligence of these ancient architects.

Also incorporated into the Egyptian culture was the science of astronomy, and with their extensive knowledge of the heavens they embraced their credence of immortality. A good example of their credence was discovered by archaeologists: this is that when a Pharaoh died his body would be placed in the King's chamber on the south face of the great pyramid. His body would be in direct alignment with Sirius, the dog star. The light from Sirius shone down the ventilating shaft onto the head of the Pharaoh, the supposition being that the soul or spirit of the Pharaoh would follow the light into the afterlife.

The Mayans were another civilisation which also attained great knowledge and wisdom. Evidence has already been presented to our world of their medical technology, and also of their advanced knowledge of the solar system. Mysterious runways and landing strips have been found in Peru and on other continents, believed to have been used for exploring outer space. Before we are tempted to be sceptical of this information we must refer to some of the transcripts in the Bible, or the ancient Indian book of Mahabharata. The Dead Sea Scrolls also make mention of the chariots of fire that ascend to the heavens. If these ancient writings are correct we might consider the Mayans had knowledge of, and contact with, extraterrestrial beings.

It has been proven that the Mayans had amazing skills in surgery, including heart transplants. Scientists in 1969 made examinations of Mayan skeletons, and discovered some of these had undergone heart and head surgery successfully. The evidence of their survival after the heart operations was the formation of a fibrous membrane called the periosteum around the bones of the aperture. Operations were also performed on part of the head, perhaps for tumours or some other reason, but never on the brain as they surmised the brain was the seat of the soul. Therefore, interfering with the brain would retard or destroy the release of the soul to afterlife.

Archaeologists have found medical instruments that had probably been used in such surgery. The materials used were mainly crystals and precision cut diamonds. These archaic methods of surgery proved to be as effective and successful as many in our modern day hospitals. I recall my Persian guide once saying through me in trance: "Nothing is new in your world, it has all been done before."

CHAPTER 14

I had been requested by a few friends to form a private development circle, and within six months two of the members were already showing the potential for clairvoyance. The energy increased rapidly in the winter months due to the colder atmospheric conditions, making it easier for the spirit entities to interpenetrate our earth plane.

Occasionally my Persian guide would control me for one or two hours and speak to the members of the circle, giving information of interest and personal. These sessions were taped, so I could listen to what had been recorded after the circle had closed for the evening. The guide would answer any questions that were asked by the members, and conversant with his information of the etheric world. I will transcribe a few of the questions asked and the information received.

One lady member asked: "Is the spirit world overcrowded because of the vast number of people that have left our earth plane?"

Without hesitation the guide replied: "No, we have no overcrowding of people, because within the confines of the universe there are many layers or planes around your earth plane. These of course are invisible to your eyes, but they are as real as your world is to you. I will explain more about the different planes. When mortals leave your earth by what you call physical death, they find their new surroundings confusing. Some adapt to the new conditions quicker than others. For instance, if a mortal has some knowledge of immortality, that person will adjust mentally to our conditions.

Our atmosphere is lighter than yours on earth, the vibrations and frequencies quicker, and your astral or spirit body will be lighter in weight than the physical form you were used to on earth. When a soul departs from your world, it will transfer to the first, second or third plane according to its spiritual development.

I will explain more about these different planes. The first or lower plane consists of individuals who desire mentally to stay close to earth for various reasons. They are what you may call earth-bound entities. Amongst these people are souls that cannot release themselves mentally from their relatives or earthly conditions, and they will attempt to attract attention in different ways. You must understand theirs is a distressing and confusing situation, as is also that of souls that inflict self-destruction of the physical body, and they also will remain mentally in this trauma until released by spirit helpers or rescue work from an earthly medium. The same applies to mortals who vacate their physical bodies as a result of an accident on earth, and it will be of interest to you that they can recreate the likeness of the physical body for only a short duration of time, and on occasion can be perceived visually by mortals close to the vicinity of their accident.

Inhabiting also this lower plane are individuals of an evil disposition, many of whom while on earth have committed crimes by design, or intent, of the assassination of one or many persons. It is correct too when said 'like attracts like', and they will remain in a mental hell until able to further their spiritual development.

Within the second plane are the halls of resting, where a large number of people will remain, comatose perhaps, for several years. They will be watched over and helped to recover from their earthly death, until they transcend to the third plane. Many of these individuals are still in a state of mental shock from the transition into our world. Also, you must remember, many of these people while on earth were dominated in their minds by the dogma of their religion, and so find it difficult to accept they have passed through the portal of our world. Others who have always been sceptical of immortality are the most difficult to heal. But when they finally accept they have left the earth plane they will transfer to the third plane".

The dialogue between the guide and circle members continued over many sessions, giving insight into the world of spirit. Listening to the information regarding the third plane, or dimension, we found it fascinating and informative.

The guide often spoke of the various halls of learning, the halls of music, art, science and many more subjects people wished to learn, according to each person's requirements. He told us of the children in spirit, and how they further their development into adults. The question of animal survival was also asked, and he replied: "Yes, they also survive the earthly death. Animals have intelligence", he said, "and maintain a natural instinct for survival. They do not question only accept the laws of nature."

The subsequent sessions throughout the next two years revealed much information regarding the etheric world. During some of these evenings the guide spoke of reincarnation, and mentioned again the continuous cycles of life for some people who return to earth to relearn from their previous mistakes. And for others the desire to be reborn to earth and further a latent talent. This makes us consider the child prodigies with their artistic perfections of music, architecture, painting etc. So, if reincarnation is a fallacy, or just wishful thinking, what other explanation can be given?

Briefly, I will transcribe some of the guide's information concerning the conditions of life in the etheric world:

"Our environment is similar to yours. We too have peaceful countryside, also gardens, but the colours are more vibrant and the flowers more fragrant than those growing on earth. We visualise, and build houses from our minds as also the food we eat. There is no mechanical transport such as on your earth. Our travelling if we wish is again obtained by mind, and our astral bodies are not an encumberment to us, as the physical body can be to you mortals.

"The weight of our astral body is two and a half ounces, in relation to your earth measurements. Also, time as you know it is different in our world, as our pace of life is slower and we have no need to regulate our movements to a timekeeper. We have no order of status over here. Who, or whatever your position may have been on earth, it will not be acknowledged. Without class distinction there is no authority to influence or change our way of life. We are as one class of people, using our mental thoughts to create the reality of a physical world. You will find no discord or animosity here, as many people from the earth plane speak to us of in their previous striving for power and financial gain, but found it did not always bring contentment or happiness".

He spoke to us at great length of the following four planes:

"You have asked me questions", he said, "but I am allowed by the higher guides to give you only a certain amount of information concerning these higher dimensions.

"The fourth and fifth planes are used for the further development of the soul. And as souls progress from one level to another, they will obtain an altered consciousness. These advanced souls are far removed from the earth plane and the people they once knew. They have entered the realms of what we call 'the soul experience', and there are certain aspects of life changes where there is no longer need for the astral body. This is called 'The second death.' The soul exists without mass, but is surrounded by a brilliant white light you call the aura."

"Individuals converse with each other only by mind. Within these higher dimensions, 'The Masters' as we call them will select the souls that will make the transition into the gateway of affinity. Other highly developed souls will be chosen to return close to your earth plane to work as your Guardians or Guides, to assist you in your spiritual development. The records of your life achievements are kept in the fifth dimension. They are known as 'The Akashic Records.'"

"These records are really a case history of every individual who exists or has lived on the earth plane. They reflect your personality, your thoughts, deeds and attitudes to everyone and everything you do while on earth. Your innermost feelings are indelibly printed on your soul."

Many of us mortals have been hurt through various experiences and found them unpleasant and disturbing to our spirit. Difficult as it may seem at the time we eventually come to terms with these situations and realise that life on earth is similar to a training ground. We learn sometimes the hard way, and within ourselves we must try not to feel bitter or angry. These are emotions that are negative and could hold us back from helping other people who are in need of love and help. And also, bad emotions can damage ourselves mentally if we let them. By this I mean we could harden our hearts and minds towards such people, but that does not solve the problem. If we hold animosity towards others, it can only cloud and darken our own mind and aura. Consequently, bad and evil thoughts could take over and destroy all principles we are working for.

Last year I had a visit from a dear friend of mine. He is a Buddhist monk, ordained by the Dalai Lama. As we sat in my peaceful garden we discussed, amongst other subjects, emotions within ourselves and towards other people.

I asked him: "When you meet people how do you help them overcome jealousy and anger?"

He replied: "I transfer from my mind a white light around such people, sending out my thoughts of love and compassion. I tell them to consider how fortunate they are to have, in both respects, their health in mind and physical body. I remind them that unfortunately in our world today there are many people who strive only for financial gain and self-advancement. But it does not bring real happiness to them. True happiness is something we find within ourselves to pass over and give to others, if only it be a smile to a stranger."

In silence we watched the river meandering along its way to the open sea. After a few moments he spoke again: "You see, Margaret, even this quiet water finds its way around these large boulders, the obstacles on its pathway home. We also will find a way to help and teach others in life."

We relate to consciousness when we think of perceptual experiences like physical body sensations - pain, pleasure, taste and the stream of thoughts that passes through our minds. Consciousness is changeable and it can be altered by a variety of factors. For example, driving a car when tired our conscious awareness and attention do not function as well as when fully awake. Our physical consciousness as we know it slips away from us during sleep state, or under an anaesthetic during an operation. But the conscious part of our brain can still operate even when unconscious.

The French philosopher Rene Descartes (1596-1650) was associated with the belief that it is possible for the mind to be conscious of its own activities directly through the process of introspection, and also relevant to Descartes' metaphysics was the distinction between mind and body, that they are entirely separate and the mind is a substance whose essence is thought alone. Reviewed experiments of psychologists Dixon and Henle (1980) proved what they believed indicated clear evidence that processing of material and psychic information can occur when unconscious. It confirms their theory when we hear or read about out-of-body experiences, astral travelling and near-death experiences.

A recent study by medical researchers found that numerous people who have suffered a cardiac arrest, and survived that ordeal, had a memory recall of that unconscious period, and they can still be aware of their surroundings although unconscious, also retaining their faculties of memory, sight and sound.

A few months ago I read an article in a newspaper about how a gentleman, while undergoing a heart by-pass operation, watched a nurse in the operating theatre. He saw her nearly drop his false teeth, and then place them in a small dish. He also heard most of the conversation between the two nurses and the surgeon.

A few days later, after he had fully recovered from the operation, he described to the consultant surgeon what he had seen and heard during the operation. "I saw my physical body on the table and I looked pretty ghastly", he said. All of what he had seen and heard was confirmed as accurate by the surgeon and the theatre nurse.

Consciousness is insubstantial, as also our mind, memory and soul. These components are invisible to the naked eye, nevertheless they are real. There are two halves to our brain, and when the stem of the higher and lower half ceases to function all consciousness, physical and mental life as we know it, has finished.

We are all aware that consciousness does not exist in a deceased body. When physical death takes place the silver cord, as I have mentioned in a previous chapter, severs completely from the physical body. The astral or spirit body is then in control of all faculties. You are then spirit and cannot re-enter the physical shell.

I think, before much time elapses, it must be seriously considered by scientists, psychoanalysts and all medics that there are dangers involved in experimenting with brain transplants.

CHAPTER 15

Emigration to another country on earth can be adventurous and exciting, and those people who embark on a new life usually gather as much information as possible beforehand about their new environment and the facilities within. In this day and age distance and contact are not a problem, and saddened as they may be by the loss of a personal contact with their friends they have the knowledge that they still exist on earth. But this is not always so for the bereaved who have experienced the pain of losing loved ones through physical death. For many people of course, physical death is final. They either have no knowledge of an afterlife, or are totally sceptical of such. Others may have a scant knowledge of the afterlife, but are still confused as to why they have not seen or heard from the people they have lost. Very often I have queries on this question and there are several answers to this.

First, it is quite possible that the spirit relatives have returned to try and make themselves known and show that they still survive. But if the mortal has no extra-sensory perception of the spirit that has returned, the barrier between them will remain. Another reason can be that the spirit relative has adjusted quickly to the new conditions after passing over, and has developed sufficiently to ascend to a higher plane.

Grief is a natural emotion when someone dies, but it becomes unnatural if prolonged over a long period of time. Grief can also mentally keep a spirit close to the earth, and continual grief can be destructive to your own spirit and health. It is good to remember the deceased with love, and remember they do still exist, but you have to let go to release them from their earthly ties. You can never make, or demand of, a spirit to return to you. Spirits will return on their own accord when, or if, they can negotiate our earth conditions.

I can recall a good example of not letting go of a deceased person. During a reading I described to the recipient an old lady who had passed over. She seemed to be very distressed, and concerned about her daughter still on the earth plane. The mother was telling me she could see her daughter sitting in a chair and holding an urn that contained her ashes.

The recipient told me after the reading that the daughter, aged forty-eight, had lived with her aged mother. "I do go in every day to visit the daughter", she told me, "but she sits, sometimes for hours, just holding the urn."

I still retain the memory of a very disturbing incident I witnessed several years ago. I was invited to lunch at a friend's house. I always enjoyed her company, and her cooking. After lunch she asked me whether I would mind walking to the cemetery with her, as she wished to place some flowers on her mother's grave. Apart from myself and my friend there was only one other person at the cemetery. It was a woman a few yards away from us. She was sitting on a small camping stool next to a grave and she was talking to herself, or so I thought.

"Who is she talking to?" I asked my friend. "Well", she said, "her mother died seven or eight years ago, but apparently she comes up here every day, rain or shine, and sits for two hours or more talking to her dead Mum, but she also brings sweets or chocolate for her and puts them on the grave." "Is she mentally ill?" I asked. "No, not clinically", she said, "it's just a case of not letting her Mum go."

The credence of the soul has been reinforced by genuine mediumistic communication, and throughout the centuries the ancients have accepted communication from the departed as proof of another world. Sadly, most of the orthodox Christian Churches today lay no claim to direct contact with the deceased. Teachings of immortality, healing and the next world are extracted from the Scriptures. Many followers of orthodox religions are told to have faith. Faith can be helpful but it does not always give positive proof in answer to our queries. The Bible is replete with parables, prophetic and cryptic messages. Prior to the transcripts in the Bible, information was given in cuneiform on clay tablets, four thousand years B.C. So why was this knowledge and wisdom concealed in such ways?

We can rightly presume that the interpretations were only intelligible to, and intended for, the initiated, people that we perhaps classed as the early prophets and they accredited their superior or supernatural knowledge to the immortals. Much of this knowledge still had to be shrouded in mystique for fear of misuse by the ignorant. It became a cult that held the keys to divine intervention and manifestations. Occultism became a secret art of esoteric science.

Although taciturn with their knowledge, parts of information on this science was leaked. Consequently, this led to misuse of the psychic arts by amateurish methods of producing psychic phenomena. (The waters of the occult run deep, and to gain complete knowledge first of all one must step in at the shallow edge). With only parts of this science, the phenomena these amateurs produced was embracing entities of the lower astral plane. Within the following decades this was termed the 'black arts', a term sometimes still used today when some people refer to spiritism as evil.

Fortunately, much of the information on the true psychic science has been gleaned from the ancient texts that were discovered over the centuries. Some of these are still hidden from the general public, in particular the Dead Sea Scrolls, which would give a deeper enlightenment into the mysteries of the esoteric if they could be deciphered. Within the Bible we find contradictory statements that can confuse us regarding spirits and immortality, but only a smattering remains of the ancient texts that give an insight of the ancient knowledge.

Most of the ancient texts were omitted when the Roman Emperor Constantine held a Church Council in the year 325 at Nicaea in Turkey. A new statement of Christian belief was drawn up, and this was called the Nicene Creed. Paganism was denounced as evil, the work of the devil, and mediums were ejected from all churches. And yet some of the Christian teachings and rituals were taken from paganism. Under the new Council the doctrine of the Trinity was established: God the Father, God the Son and God the Holy Ghost.

The Nicene Creed was modified by the Council of Constantinople in 381, and ideas of Greek and Roman philosophy were introduced into the Christian churches. The Romans eventually adopted the Christian faith, becoming known as the Christian Roman Church.

Even in our present day world some of the old traditions and beliefs are still observed. A deceased person is generally left three days before burial or cremation, the supposition being that it takes three days for the soul to vacate the physical body. With this, we are reminded of the resurrection of Jesus, after three days.

In many of the eastern countries the dead were disposed of more quickly, partly for hygienic reasons, the body or bodies being placed on a funeral pyre and burnt. The main reason was that fire is cleansing and burns upwards towards the heavens. The soul, therefore, would leave the physical body quickly. Two different methods of bodily disposal, but both laying claim to immortality.

The Mousterian Neanderthal man used some of the earliest methods of ritual burials. They interred their dead in trenches that were dug inside caves. The corpses were painted over with red ochre and bound into a foetal position, representing the likeness of an infant in the womb (ready to be born). Food and weapons were also placed near them. Their credence of immortality was furthered by recurring symbols painted on the walls of the cave. Some of these symbols depicted the mysteries of the occult and primitive magic, their magic being only the foretelling of future events. In our modern age we would classify these people as natural mediums. The word 'magic' was originally derived from the priests of the Zoroastrian religion of ancient Persia.

During the 12th century A.D. a deeper interest in the esoteric arts was growing, together with the renewal of paganism, pagan meaning country folk, which in reality they were. Gentle and quiet in their ways they lived their lives to blend with all of nature. They were also intelligent, with their knowledge of astrology and agriculture. It was customary for them to sow their seeds in late spring during a full moon, which later on always produced a good harvest.

Certain herbs were also gathered under a full moon, and used fresh or dried to cure ailments and for culinary use. Most of these pagans had the gift of clairvoyance and spiritual healing, by touch or thought. They became known as the wise people or the "Wicca". Eventually their craft became known as Witchcraft.

During the 15th - 17th centuries the Christian Church persecuted the witches. People were paid by the Church first of all to round up and destroy as many cats as they could find, cats being classed as the witches' 'familiar spirit.' This was mainly the cause of the plague of London in the year 1665. Owing to the absence of the cats the narrow streets of London became overrun with vermin. The Church again paid people to hunt out the witches. All were accused of black magic, and cruelly tortured until confessions were wrung from them.

In the early stages of their punishment the witches would be securely tied up and thrown into deep water, where they were left for several hours. If they survived it proved they were innocent. Needless to say, the possibility of survival was nil. Death by drowning was perhaps a merciful release. Their persecutors, realising this was too easy a death, decided on hanging or better still burning them alive. The witch-hunt craze spread indiscriminately across the European boundaries, and many thousands of witches were unjustly accused of practising black craft and put to death.

Gradually doubts began to appear in the witch-hunters, minds as to whether an injustice was being done, as many of these witches refused to recant before they were burnt. Consequently, England abolished witch-hunts and persecutions in 1684, albeit from time to time unlawful burnings of witches were still practised until the beginning of the 18th century.

The witch-hunts were a designed massacre on the part of the Christian Church. Was it because they posed such a threat to the teachings of the Church that they were hunted down and killed? I doubt that. The Wicca were white witches, peace-loving and with natural gifts.

A book on witchcraft was written in 1486 by two Dominican monks. The book was called "Malleus Maleficarum". It was the ultimate authority for every judge, and Catholic or Protestant priest. In the book instructions were given on how to dispose of a witch, the verdict usually being by burning.

The term 'witches' never really faded away and many of today's mediums are still classed as witches. During the years between 1930 and

1940 mediums would be accused of fraud and practising the black arts, punishable by imprisonment as Spiritualism was considered illegal. In 1950 a genuine medium, a Mrs Helen Duncan, was brought to court to face charges of fraud under the old witchcraft act. She was cleared of any fraud or black magic, and a private member's bill was passed in Parliament in 1950. This bill legalised mediumship and is still known as the 'Fraudulent Medium's Bill.'

I remember an amusing true story about a witch that was told to me years ago by an uncle who used to live in Hoddesdon, Hertfordshire. Hoddesdon was a rural village in 1912, and my uncle and a few of his school friends were aged ten at the time when this incident with the witch occurred.

On the outskirts of the village, an old woman lived by herself in a thatched cottage. She was regarded by the local people as a witch, and feared by many of them. There was no reason for their fear, as she helped them with herbal medicines when they were sick.

My uncle and the small group of boys would on occasion walk past her cottage with the intent of teasing her by throwing small stones at her front door. She never reprimanded them, but would place a box of apples for them outside her gate.

Over a period of three weeks she had politely asked the local chimney sweep if he would sweep her chimney, but he would always make excuses telling her he would do it the following week. Of course he had no intention of cleaning it, as he was terrified of her.

One day the boys noticed the chimney sweep coming along the lane with his horse and cart. As they watched the witch came out of her cottage and stood in the centre of the lane, blocking the sweep's way. She asked him again to sweep her chimney. "I have money to pay you," she said, "and I won't harm you in any way".

Once again he made an excuse. She never answered but stood in front of the horse, speaking in a low voice. The sweep shouted to the horse to move on, but the horse could not move. The witch had hypnotised him. The sweep tried all methods to get the horse moving, but to no avail. "Now", said the witch, "you had better come in and sweep my chimney for me, if you don't the horse will remain here all day unmovable."

Shaking like a leaf the sweep collected his brushes from the cart, and duly swept the chimney. She paid him the money that was due, and as he climbed back into the cart she said: "Next time I ask you to clean my chimney don't make excuses!" With that she again spoke softly to the horse, and within two seconds the horse was back to normal.

Hypnotism is accepted today as being extremely useful for relief, and cure, in various health problems, especially for people who need help for stress, pain or fear. Hypnosis is an altered state of consciousness, and can vary from a light to a deeper trance state. Suggestion is usually used when a person is being hypnotised, although a light trance state can be achieved by oneself by relaxation and without suggestion. Again, under hypnosis, past lives may be recalled. This is known as regression. From the subconscious mind, latent memories of places or people may be remembered.

During sleep state, or hypnosis, the astral body is slightly separated from the physical body. Hypnosis should not be classed as pertaining to the occult. When genuine mediums are controlled by a spirit guide, no suggestion or hypnosis has previously been proposed. Once the astral body has withdrawn from the physical form, it will still be attached to the physical by the silver cord and will feel any pain imposed on it, but the physical body will feel absolutely nothing.

Years ago in London I was fortunate to witness an experiment on a genuine trance medium, regarding withdrawal of the astral body. Two investigators of psychic science were present, also myself and a gentleman of known repute for honesty. The experiment was held in a small room in broad daylight. Five chairs were placed in a small circle, and another empty chair was placed the other side of the room.

The trance medium was told nothing about the experiment but was asked only, if he did go into a trance state, would he try to project his astral body into the empty chair. It had previously been agreed with the investigators that if the medium did manage to project his astral they would test him by pricking his arm several times with a pin.

Nearly twenty minutes later the medium was in deep trance. The two investigators went over to the medium and pricked his bare arms three times. There was no involuntary movement from the medium. They then went over to the empty chair and pricked where they supposed the two astral arms would be. The chair then moved violently as if an unseen person had received a sudden shock.

Fifteen minutes later the medium had returned from his trance with no ill effects. The test proved that the astral body did react to the pin pricks as it was a short distance away from the physical body but still attached by the silver cord. But if the medium had been under a heavy anaesthetic as used in operations, the astral body would be a greater distance away and would not feel any pain.

CHAPTER 16

Halfway down the long driveway I stopped and looked back at the 'House.' It was my last day of work there, I had retired. The staff had prepared a surprise buffet for me which was attended by the Inspectors and Advisors. I had been given a large bouquet of flowers and cards from all the staff. It had been a lovely surprise, but in myself I was feeling sad because I knew I would miss my colleagues, as likewise the spirits that still resided in the 'House.'

The evening sun was casting a crimson glow over the windows of the 'House'. In a few hours time the 'House' would be standing dark and gaunt in the moonlight, with only the two stone lions standing sentinel each side of the large front door. Walking homewards, my thoughts a mixture of feelings, I pondered on how I should now use my free time. Having passed my examinations for teaching floristry, I could now embark on a new career if I wished to do so. It was a question of finding time, as many requests for private readings were still being made.

By the time I had reached home I had decided that in a fortnight's time I would travel to Brussels to visit my son. It would be relaxing and a change of environment, also giving me the opportunity to meet up with some friends again. The spirit people I would leave behind in Cornwall, or so I thought.

Three days after I had retired I started to sort out a few casual clothes to take on my holiday. Why was I doing this so early, I thought? Suddenly there was loud crash on my bedroom wall. There was no normal explanation for this noise. The time, I noticed, was two-thirty p.m. My husband had heard nothing unusual, and he checked the loft upstairs just in case something falling might have caused the crash.

The 'phone rang at three-thirty p.m. The call was from Brussels. It was a call from my son's friend, telling me my son had been involved in a serious car crash and was in hospital, unconscious. Could I come over to Brussels as soon as possible? I was fortunate to obtain a booking for the Eurostar the following day, and finally reached the hospital at nine-thirty p.m. The hospital staff had been advised I was travelling from England and permission had been given to allow me to see my son, however late the hour. He had regained consciousness, but his condition was still critical. I remained in Brussels for six weeks, and during this time he had undergone several operations. But I knew he would survive and walk again.

During this traumatic period I experienced two psychic incidents that I can clearly recall even today. For the first three weeks I stayed with a friend in the Chaussee d'Ixelles in Brussels. She rented a very nice self-contained flat, and it was within easy reach of the hospital. One evening after visiting my son in hospital, my friend and I stopped in the Grand Place for a coffee. It was not late when we reached the apartment, and we both retired for the night to our separate rooms. My room overlooked the busy avenue. I turned off the bedroom light and stood by the window for a while, watching the constant stream of traffic.

A nagging pain in my left groin, which I had felt coming on during the evening, started to increase. For the next hour I walked about the room, trying to will the pain to go away. Unfortunately, I had left my toilet bag in my friend's bedroom, so I had no access to a pain killer. I presumed my friend was asleep by now and I felt I could not disturb her, as she had to go to work in the morning. From past experience I knew the pain had to be Diverticulitis (an inflammation in the intestinal tract). I climbed into bed and tried to relax, but could not sleep, knowing it would take at least three days before the pain left me.

After five minutes I heard a slight noise in the room, and sat up in bed. Looking around I could see every detail, as the room was illuminated by the orange street lights from outside. The solid figure of a lady walked towards me. She was smiling and I sensed love and compassion from her. She wore the black habit of a nun, and I could see a silver crucifix as she leaned over me. I felt no fear as she placed her hands on me, and a sensation of a deep warmth entered my body. I remembered nothing else until I awoke next morning. All pain had gone.

I was cautious when I questioned my friend in the evening, asking her whether she had experienced anything strange in the apartment. "Well", she said, "I definitely have heard footsteps other than mine, and once or twice caught a glimpse of a lady wearing black. Why do you ask?" I told her of my experience. She was interested, and suggested that as tomorrow was Saturday we could visit the Abbey at the end of the avenue. "I'll make some enquiries as to any Sisters of Mercy who may have lived around here."

The Abbey stood in a very peaceful setting overlooking a large lake with weeping-willow trees along the banks. We waited until the morning service was over, and then went inside. Our first enquiry brought no positive response to our questions. We were starting to feel a little despondent, but as we walked back to the main door my friend walked over to an old man with white hair. He was lighting candles in a small alcove. Speaking rapidly in French the old man was pointing towards the avenue. I gathered information of some sort might be forthcoming.

My friend was smiling as she came towards me. "The old man remembers his grandfather talking about a convent not too far from here", she said, "and it was partly destroyed by a fire. It was many years ago now, and eventually new houses and shops were built on the old site." We could only assume the Sister of Mercy had at some time lived close to my friend's apartment, and as she was spiritually advanced she could descend to our earth plane to give help and healing to mortals, her vocation the same as when she lived on earth.

For the last three weeks of my visit to Belgium I stayed with another friend in a small town called Nivelles, on the outskirts of Brussels. The house she owned was quite large. She had had much work done in alterations to the interior before she moved in, which I thought was a pleasing improvement but apart from that there was an overpowering atmosphere in the house that I felt was not desirable. This was not due to her presence as she was a nice person, but I sensed strongly there was an unseen entity that perhaps resented the alterations to the house, or any new owners within.

Two days after I had settled in with my friend I saw the entity: a large, burly man with an unkempt appearance. I sensed someone watching me as I undressed for bed. He was standing by the open bedroom door. "Who are you?" I asked. He answered me speaking quickly in French, at the same time gesturing with his hands that he wanted me to leave, presumably the house. I told him I was a guest here, and it was he who should leave as he was for some reason earthbound. "Your time on earth has finished, please accept this fact and go forward now to a higher plane, you will find peace at last." There was a bewildered look on his face and he started to become almost transparent, and then he was gone. I never felt or saw him again during my visit, and the atmosphere in the house felt lighter.

The following week my friend related this experience to her next-door neighbour. "How strange", she said. "My two children have never slept properly at night since we moved in here a year ago. It's only these last few nights they have slept peacefully without waking up before morning." Further information regarding the unwelcome entity was that the previous owner of my friend's house had been an alcoholic. He had died by falling down the stairs, while under the influence of drink.

My son was allowed to leave the hospital a week before I was due to travel back to England. He was walking on crutches, and his eyesight was slightly impaired. His employers in Brussels informed him they would pay his salary for a year until he could return to work.

Travelling back to England I knew I would have a backlog of readings to do. But I tried to dismiss them from my mind, which was just as well as a medium's job is not to presume what a person has come for, and every reading is personal information for each recipient. And so, perhaps, I would have felt slightly perturbed if I had known beforehand that I was to come face to face during a reading with a young girl who had been murdered.

A very attractive girl was sitting opposite me at the table, she had dark hair, her face devoid of any make-up. She smiled at me now and again, although I felt she was tense and apprehensive. But after ten minutes she relaxed and was alert to the information I was passing over to her. My recipient was wearing a pink blouse and a grey skirt, but as I looked at her clairvoyantly I could see her dressed in a nurse's uniform.

"You are a hospital nurse", I told her. "Yes", she replied. "There is a young lady from spirit standing at the side of you. She also was a nurse when on the earth plane. She tells me her name is Sarah, and she is very much like you in appearance. You could be sisters, but she says you and her were just good friends." Again she confirmed this information.

"I am now being shown a small dark pathway with tall bushes on either side. A nurse in uniform is walking down the pathway." The recipient put a hand over her mouth. "Oh, my God!" she said. "Do you want me to go on with the reading?" I asked. "Yes please. I'm alright", she replied. "I see a tallish man come out from behind the bushes. He has something in his hand, a scarf I think, which he is tightening around her neck. The man disappears back into the bushes, and the nurse is left lying on the pathway. The girl who died by strangulation was called Sarah, and she is here with you today, although in spirit. She is not earthbound and has come back to give her love to you. One last message from her. She says - 'I always told you Eric was a nutter. I proved to be right, didn't I?'"

The reading finished on the hour, and of her own accord she explained the story to me. Two years ago Eric had been my recipient's boy-friend. She said he had always been possessive and jealous. Several times she had tried to break off her relationship with him, but he kept threatening her that he would kill her if she found someone else.

"I met a really nice chap", she said. "He was kind and considerate. He also accepted the different shifts I had to work at the hospital. It was eleven fifteen p.m. when Sarah and I finished work. We started to walk down the pathway to the nurses' home, we were both tired and ready for a hot drink and bed. I suddenly remembered I had left my black purse in my locker instead of putting it back in my handbag. 'You go on', I said to Sarah, 'it won't take me long to go back for it' But unfortunately it took me longer than I thought, because one of the night nurses asked me if I could have a quick look at a patient's bad leg as she thought it looked septic.

"Nearly twenty minutes later when I came out of the hospital I saw three police cars. I could not take the short cut down the pathway as there was a yellow tape across it. A policeman stood in front of it. 'Sorry Miss', he said, 'you can't go down there.' I asked why, and he replied: 'A young girl has been murdered.'"

"Was it your friend?" I asked. "Yes it was Sarah. I wish with all my heart I had not gone back for my purse."

After she had cried for a while, she went on to tell me her ex-boy friend Eric had confessed to the police that he had strangled Sarah. "I killed the wrong girl by mistake. It should have been Debbie, they looked so much alike."

I have given numerous readings to people from all walks of life, and within these pages I have transcribed just a few that the reader may find interesting. I feel I have given much in the way of proof and comfort to those who have been in need of genuine help, and perhaps released from them part of the trauma of losing a loved one. I am grateful the spirit people have used me as an intermediary between the two worlds, and I feel my time on this earth plane has been of some use to others.

Being clairvoyant and clairaudient from an early age, I became adjusted to the fact that I could sense and see what many people could not. These psychic experiences lessened slightly through my teens, but resumed again strongly at the age of twenty. They have remained with me ever since.

Spirit people cannot be called back to us, they come to us of their own accord when and if they can. It must be remembered that many spirits have developed further to higher levels, so the learning is progressive. The spirits who can come back to us are well aware of our presence and problems, and will advise us through genuine readings, intuition or even in our sleep state.

I started to question myself: why was I reluctant to believe that these people I could see and hear could still be alive after physical death? How and where did they live, and how was it possible they could appear as solid as us mortals at times, but able to walk through closed doors or walls? I knew from personal experience their bodies were firm and warm, I had at times touched them. Within seconds they could become transparent and vanish. Therefore my enquiring mind and curiosity started to prompt me into research, and prove whether all mortals and animals survived earthly death. If my findings proved contrary to this, then I could honestly claim that all I, and other people, had seen had to be a psychological illusion.

I learned from science that all matter looks and feels solid to us, but in reality it's density is composed of imperceptibly small units of atomic particles that are at rest until an external force initiates motion. These microscopic objects are transient composites of atoms, and when life departs from living matter - whatever it may be - it will start to decay. The timbers and various other building materials that are used for our requirements will still contain atomic particles, perhaps for centuries, until they finally crumble or rot away. Consequently, spirits have no problem moving through density as they visualise the object as particles of living energy.

The spirit guides have told us, in their world there are seven planes, sometimes spoken of as dimensions, each one supported by its own energy field and gravity. They are tuned to higher frequencies and have a larger range of vibrations than our world. They also spoke of their atmosphere being lighter and colder (this accounts for the sudden lowering of temperature around us when the spirits come close to us), although they easily adjust to our earthly environment.

Quite often when I was in a trance state my Persian guide would invite the members of the circle to ask questions if they so wished, so that much information from the guide was given on life in the world of spirit. He told us of their use of power and energy of the mind. "By mind we envisage what we need", he said, "whether it be food or a house. We build from the atoms and movement of the subatomic particles, and so we achieve the density that you have on earth. If you could see your earth plane with our vision you would view it as a vibrating globe of energy. You would then understand how all these elements and energy patterns are natural forces in the ether, and form in all living things including your body, but cannot be seen with a physical perception".

The guide gave us much more in-depth and valuable information regarding the structure of the spirit world. Listening to the tape afterwards we realised his knowledge of quantum physics was greater than ours.

Over a period of six months the guide answered many questions regarding the spirit world, our earth-plane and also the eventual emergence of recent mortals in the realm of spirit. He spoke of their world being superior to ours. "Our land is similar to your environment, with many rivers and forests, fields that are prolific with natural wild flowers, the colours of which are more vibrant than those on earth. This is because our atmosphere is pure, with no pollution. Everything is tangible to us, as real as your world is to you. Our senses are stronger than yours and more sensitive to the aromas around us. Life force in all plants and vegetation does not decay as you know it, there is only a short time of transition until the full life force is renewed. The infrastructure of our world we construct from our minds, and it is not destroyed as on your earth. We are saddened as we see the devastation that is being done by mortals on your earth-plane. You have contamination of poisons in the oceans, and the air you breathe is no longer pure. The vast forests that at one time gave off a life force of their own for mortals' benefit are slowly diminishing. Even the food that you eat has not the quality for the nourishment of your bodies. All that is natural on your earth-plane is being ignored, perhaps for the constant pursuit of material gain which in time will only bring devastation and disease to your earth-plane."

During one of our lengthy sessions valuable information was given by the guide on the transition from the earth-plane into the world of spirit.

"What you mortals call death is really just a journey, passing from one world into the next one in a sub-, or unconscious, state that is peaceful. This state of so-called death is not to be feared, more so perhaps, the fear of any illness your physical body may be afflicted with before you enter our realm. We are aware that many mortals have experienced near death and have been conscious of following the white light through the tunnel. This is correct but, if their term on earth has not been completed, their silver cord that is still adjoined to the physical will return to its earthly surroundings. The spirit within you is the only moving, working and thinking part of your physical body. When the spirit is naturally ready to leave the physical, the shell or outer covering of you will be left on earth. It is then your astral body will continue to follow the white light through what you call "the tunnel", but in reality it is similar to a vortex, and the journey being transitory.

"When you mortals eventually enter into our world you will realise your mental characteristics, your inclinations and your passions are no more changed immediately on the decay of your physical body than they are today. Remember, you are a spirit now, but encased in a physical body."

We were also enlightened on the many aspectual ways of life in the next world, which is a VAST subject, and would take much time to transcribe within these pages. We learned again from the guide that as a person progresses spiritually from a lower level they will ascend to the other spheres of spirit. (This is called the second death, and reference to this can be found in the Holy Bible).

Much more valuable information was disclosed during this session of one and a half hours. As he left us he said: "We also learn from our higher masters of spirit. There is a supreme power and ruling force which pervades the boundless universe".

Over the years with my research into parapsychology the jigsaw puzzle was nearly complete, although many questions will remain unanswered, and perhaps that is meant to be until I myself become an immortal, and then the whole picture will be completed. So why was I reluctant to believe in an afterlife?

I think, like so many people, I could not accept the fact that the deceased could be resurrected from an earthly physical state. Also, it was inconceivable that another invisible world, or worlds, existed, other than our earth-plane. And how was it possible these people we called spirits could appear to us incarnate?

My curiosity had prompted me into deep thought about the many psychic experiences I had known during my childhood, and continued throughout my life. I recall how I had asked the spirits questions, and without hesitation had been given the answers that proved to be accurate. Also, during my employment in the large 'House', I had almost demanded that the spirits show themselves to me and other people. My requests were granted at various times, and in different rooms in the 'House'. All these manifestations of the spirits were not illusory, nor a creative figment of my imagination. These were real or, (as I prefer to them), the ethereal people.

My quest and research had not been in vain. I had proved the authenticity of these people that had once inhabited the 'House', also the numerous spirits that visited me over the years. I thought it appropriate to quote these few lines of the authoress, Louisa May Alcott -

"I think immortality is the passing of a soul through many lives or experiences, and such as are truly lived, used and learned, to help on to the next, each growing richer, happier and higher, carrying with it only the real memories of what has gone before."

There is no chasm between the material or spiritual worlds. They blend imperceptibly into each other. In reality the material world is only a visible form of the finer elements we call spiritual. And if we could see our world from a great distance, we would probably liken it to a pinhead compared to the galaxies, planets, the other suns and moons that exist in the whole of the universe, also the celestial bodies that abide there. These living and vibrating energies are all around and within ourselves, and throughout the whole of the universe.

The laws of spirit are a respecter of your motives in working with, and for them. If your intentions are to give comfort, proof or healing to those in need of such, the spirit people will make contact with you. But if your motive is only for financial gain or self-advancement, the spiritual faculties and finer perceptive powers will be withdrawn from you. There are many individuals who have these latent spiritual powers. When and if you develop them in accordance with the laws of spirit, all energy used from your physical body will be replenished by the spirit guides.

I would suggest to all people who seek proof and enlightenment of immortality: accept what you find as true information and reject what is suspect. Unfortunately, there are many who claim the gift of clairvoyance or healing, their motives being only monetary or self-importance. It saddens me to hear of these people, as there are so many individuals in our world who are distressed and lonely at the loss of loved ones.

In his teachings Jesus said to the people: "Seek and ye shall find." Bear in mind his words as you search for enlightenment and genuine proof of the afterlife. But in your search try to keep an open mind, and try not to be too sceptical. Be your own judge and jury, and always remember it is the mediums' job to tell you what they are receiving from spirit. Avoid those who may say to you: "Ask me a question, and I will give you an answer." I am referring to personal questions that may give a suspect medium an insight into your way of life, or relations and the loss of loved ones. Be wise, and do not divulge any information before or during a reading. When you are given accurate proof during the session, give your acknowledgement to the medium with a: "Yes, I do understand, thank you."

There are many genuine mediums who have the gift of clairvoyance and healing, etc., not all work within a Spiritualist church. They are honest and sincere towards the people they help. It is the odd ones we come across occasionally who give Spiritualism a bad name by the pretence of a psychic gift they do not have. But to ask questions about the after-life and gain knowledge of this vast subject will open up for you a greater perspective of the Universe and the invisible worlds around us.

Fear of the unknown is caused mainly by the lack of knowledge and ignorance. I have been surprised at times to hear or read that many people think the subject of the occult is combined with witchcraft and devil worship. This misconception is again based on ignorance. Spiritualists oppose black witchcraft as it is the complete opposite to all spiritual teachings and the principles of good thoughts and deeds. People tend to place the word magic with the occult. The interpretation of magic is believed to originate from the ancient Magi, the famous secret society of Persian magicians. The Persian Magi were adept in their knowledge of astrology and the paranormal. This esoteric science was enigmatic. The knowledge and wisdom gained was mainly in symbolic forms, as also used by the Chaldeans of ancient Babylonia. Their mystical and ritualistic writings are also related to the interpretations of the occult.

This written collection is called the Cabala, which means in Hebrew 'The Hidden Wisdom'. Mysticism is as old as humanity and can be found in virtually all cultures and religions. It eludes definition and a logical analysis, as it belongs to the intangible.

I know I have been fortunate in my life to sense, see and speak to the spirit people that come close to me, and also to have experienced the phenomena they can produce as evidence of survival. Their description of the next world is incomparable as to ours in regard to light and their environment. They have told us they do not feel or experience pain. Pain, they tell us, is of a physical nature only. However, we do know that during a reading they can, through the medium, produce the symptoms they themselves endured on earth. These pains are only momentary for the medium, but do give proof of the spirit's identity.

I feel it wise to express here two warnings. The first, if contemplating joining a development circle, make certain the medium is genuine, and that the circle is protected from all bad thoughts. If you feel there is a lack of harmony amongst the group, it would be well to politely ask that person, or persons, to withdraw from your group. My second warning is for people who suffer from depression or pain. Amongst many of these people there are those who contemplate suicide. To terminate your physical life before a natural death will not ensure your entry into the proper light world of spirit. For these unhappy people who do take their own lives will retain the consequences of their suicide perhaps for months or years, and will continue to remain on the lowest level of the next world, until the astral spirit has been helped and recovers from being forced out of the physical body.

When our relatives or friends leave this earth-plane, for whatever reason, it is natural that we are saddened and grieve for our loss. But to grieve for a long time is no help for that person in spirit, for our sad thoughts and tears will also grieve that person and hold them back from their new life.

The survival of physical death is a reality, it has been proven to me as likewise many thousands of people. Stories of ghosts and spirits have prevailed in every age and every nation, and have been told since human history was recorded in writing or tradition. They are based on truth and reality.

I belong to no particular denomination, and under no illusions that I am regarded as a pagan, perhaps for my contradictory thoughts on orthodox religions. But I am content with that. My garden is my temple where I find peace and enlightenment with the natural energies around me.

And whatever your nationality or creed may be, I pray that the love and blessings of spirit be with each and every one of you.

Margaret.